Where Alpha

Meets Omega

Mythology of the Constellations, Space Exploration, & Astrology

SONRISA EAST

Copyright

Disclosures

Many issues covered in this book contain rapidly changing factual knowledge. Although the author and publisher have made every effort to ensure that the information in this book was correct at press time, the author and publisher do not assume and hereby disclaim any liability to any party for any loss, damage, or disruption caused by errors or omissions, whether such errors or omissions result from negligence, accident, or any other cause. Likewise, this book is not intended as a substitute for the medical advice of physicians or psychological practitioners. The reader should regularly consult a physician or a counselor in matters relating to his/her physical and mental health, particularly about any symptoms that may require diagnosis or medical attention.

Where Alpha Meets Omega

Contents

Copyright 1

Disclosures 2

Recorded History 11

Constellations of Stars 17

   When were stars first assembled as constellations? ..20

   The first recordings of a constellation may have been
   as long as 17,300 years ago 20

   The first verified records of constellations were in the
   long-vanished civilizations of Sumeria and Akkadia in
   the Middle East nearly 6,000 years ago 21

   Star chart and constellations in the Far East about
   2,500 years ago. 23

   The ancient Greek constellations from about 2,300
   years ago. 25

   Second-hand knowledge and Star Catalogs from early
   Ancient Greece. 27

   Third-hand knowledge and Constellation Maps from
   later Ancient Greece. 28

   The 48 "Classical Constellations" from Ptolemy about
   1,900 years ago. 30

      FORMALHAUT 31

      BETA TAURI. 32

      NU BOÖTES. 32

   The 88 "Modern Constellations" 33

If there are 88 Constellations, why twelve Zodiac Signs?
.... 38

For now, what makes a constellation a Zodiac Constellation? 39

Changes from the original Zodiac symbols. 43

CONCEPTUAL symbols. 44

GLYPH symbols...44

The most dramatic changes in Zodiac symbolism are the types of beings associated with the signs............45

Space Exploration in the 21st Century 50

The short road from exploration to colonization..........52

Zodiac Constellations Reconsidered, Again...................54

THE CONSTELLATION OF ARIES...............................56

How Aries was seen in antiquity. 57

What we know about the constellation of Aries today. ...63

Multiple stars in Aries with exoplanets. 64

Other atypical features of Aries....................................65

New insights into the meaning of Aries? 66

THE CONSTELLATION OF TAURUS............................69

How Taurus was seen in antiquity...................................70

What we know about the constellation of Taurus today. 74

New insights into the meaning of Taurus? 77

THE CONSTELLATION OF GEMINI..............................80

How Gemini was seen in antiquity..................................81

What we know about the Constellation of Gemini today. 85

Much of Gemini is easily visible. 87

Double stars, binary stars, and exoplanets in Gemini.88

Gemini is filled with meteor showers...........................89

Other notable findings in Gemini.................................90

Gemini's connection with discovery. 91

New insights into the meaning of Gemini? 93

THE CONSTELLATION OF CANCER 95

How Cancer was seen in antiquity. 96

What we know about the Constellation of Cancer today.
....102

    The brightest star in Cancer is the rare Al Tarf. 103

    Other exoplanets in the constellation of Cancer. 104

    Cancer is filled with extremely distant sky objects and
    star clusters...105

    Other interesting findings about Cancer. 107

New insights into the meaning of Cancer? 108

THE CONSTELLATION OF LEO 111

How Leo was seen in antiquity. 112

    Two competing Greek myths of Leo. 113

    The myth of Heracles/Hercules and the Nemean Lion.
   113

    The myth of Pyramus, Thisbe, the mulberry tree, and
    the lion. 117

What we know about the Constellation of Leo today....120

    The constellation of Leo is visually prominent in the
    sky...121

    Leo has a large number of exoplanets in it. 122

    Strange anomalies in the constellation of Leo. 123

    Meteor showers in Leo..124

New insights into the meaning of Leo?.........................125

THE CONSTELLATION OF VIRGO..............................128

How Virgo was seen in antiquity...................................129

    Multiple female deities have been associated with Virgo
    over the eons. 131

What we know about the Constellation of Virgo today. 136

Virgo is filled with exoplanets....................................137

A bit more on Spica and the other brightest stars in Virgo...138

Other findings of significance in Virgo................139

Galaxy clusters & black holes in Virgo....................140

New insights into the meaning of Virgo? 142

THE CONSTELLATION OF LIBRA.............................145

How Libra was seen in antiquity. 146

Themis. 147

The Horai. 149

The Moirai. 151

Atalanta...154

Astraea...157

Other Goddesses Associated with Libra.................159

A Specific Note about the "New" Constellation of Libra. 160

The Apparently Forgotten Contribution of Scorpio to the Constellation of Libra. 161

And, inching closer to modern times.........................162

What we know about the constellation of Libra today. .163

The oldest star in the universe is located in Libra.....165

New insights into the meaning of Libra?.....................168

THE CONSTELLATION OF SCORPIO.......................172

How Scorpio was seen in antiquity..............................173

What we know about the constellation of Scorpio today. 178

Scorpio is full of bright stars.......................................180

ANTARES. 180

The other major stars in Scorpio..............................182

The two Al Niyats in Scorpio. 185

Scorpio contains two meteor showers. 186

The Fastest Known Nova is in Scorpio. 187

Scorpio contains four deep sky or Messier objects...188

New insights into the meaning of Scorpio? 189

THE CONSTELLATION OF OPHIUCHUS...................192

How Ophiuchus was seen in antiquity...........................193

Asclepius in ancient Greek mythology. 194

Apparently there is life after death, even for a god. ...199

What we know about the constellation of Ophiuchus today..202

Notable stars in Ophiuchus.......................................203

A particularly intriguing newly found exoplanet.........206

The recurrent novae in Ophiuchus.............................207

A rare superbubble in Ophiuchus. 207

New insights into the meaning of Ophiuchus. 209

THE CONSTELLATION OF SAGITTARIUS 214

How Sagittarius was seen in antiquity. 215

What we know about the constellation of Sagittarius today..220

The Black Hole at the center of our universe is in Sagittarius. 223

Nebulae & Galaxies in Sagittarius. 225

New insights into the meaning of Sagittarius?..............226

THE CONSTELLATION OF CAPRICORN...................229

How Capricorn was seen in antiquity. 230

The Sea-Goat mythology of Capricorn dates back more than 3,000 years. 231

The Sea-Goat persisted through most of Greek mythology..231

The Sea-Goat was lost by modern times..................233

What we know about the constellation of Capricorn today.
....234

The brightest stars in Capricorn.............................235

Unusual deep space objects found in Capricorn. 237

New insights into the meaning of Capricorn?..............238

From our new science..239

THE CONSTELLATION OF AQUARIUS....................241

How Aquarius was seen in antiquity...........................242

Other Greek and Roman mythologies about the
constellation of Aquarius...244

The concept of the constellation of Aquarius in other
parts of the ancient world..245

What we know about the constellation of Aquarius today.
....248

The brightest stars in Aquarius. 249

Aquarius and the star Fomalhaut..............................250

Other interesting "occupants" of the constellation of
Aquarius..250

Potential homes for man in Aquarius. 251

New insights into the meaning of Aquarius. 253

THE CONSTELLATION OF PISCES 255

How Pisces was seen in antiquity. 256

What we know about the constellation of Pisces today.
....263

The main stars found in Pisces................................264

Pisces' exoplanets. 265

Deep sky objects of interest in the constellation of
Pisces. 266

Other particularly curious findings about Pisces.......267

New insights into the meaning of Pisces? 269

So how does this "change" our modern concept of the Zodiac—or should it?...272

Does the Zodiac change over time? 275

Should the Zodiac change over time? Or, maybe more to the point, will it change?.......................................275

Parting thoughts from the author. 277

Author's Request. 280

Recorded History

W̲e do not know with certainty when "life" began on Earth.

It seems every few years we find new evidence of earlier and earlier "life." And the rapid increase of our knowledge over the 20th and 21st centuries of other solar systems, galaxies, and even planets circling around other stars in other galaxies strain Earth science to the very edge of science fiction. Even if we were 100 percent rock-certain what constitutes life on Earth, our certainty of life in another atmosphere, gravity, and possible chemical makeup is frail at best.

But of course, it is not just life that is a fragile concept. We have an even more difficult time defining "human" life.

Our scientists have a fairly clear definition of *Homo sapiens,* which many of us assume is a word synonymous with humans. But science does not agree as to the "human-ness" or *degree* of human-ness of a whole series of pre-Homo sapiens beings we have found the remains of. Each decade our archaeologists seem to be getting closer to clarity. Our science seems to be growing towards a consensus. But we still are not certain of that magic moment of "human." Or even of "life."

Our history is unclear. But our *recorded* history gives us some definite road maps.

It is that recorded history that we are going to consider in this book.

Some of Earth's earliest records are written in symbols or pictures. Some are carved, some chiseled, some painted, some built. Most of these ancient records cannot be precisely dated. A few of them can be carbon-dated to give a general idea of age. But ancient records of information and ideas can be dated only to when something was recorded, not to when the information or the ideas that were recorded first arose.

12

So as we look through some of our most ancient records, we need to keep in mind that any date we may have goes back to the recording. It does not show us the actual earliest manifestation or how long the information had been known or in use at the moment that particular record was made.

And although we can see where the record is located, we have no idea where the information or ideas that were recorded came from. Or how many other places the same information traveled to.

Too far away? Let's look at it a different way.

This is only a story. But it could be real.

Traveling in Greece in 1967, I ventured up to an old chapel on Skaros Rock on the island of Santorini. And as I stood looking out over the Aegean Sea, I was deeply moved by the ancient stones I was standing upon. I deeply felt how very, very old the stones beneath my feet were and how many lives had touched them. I wondered how many eyes had looked out over that beautiful blue and how many ears had listened to the gentle lapping of the waves on the cliffs far below. I was overcome with emotion. The rhythmic waves against the ancient rock lit my imagination and almost brought me to tears. I sat down on the rocks and pulled out a tablet and a pen from my pack. And as I sat there, with tear-filled eyes, I wrote about what I was listening to, seeing, and feeling. It was sort of a letter, sort of a poem. But I signed it anyway and put the date beneath my signature. The closing of the letter said:

SONRISA
20 April 1967 .

Since it really wasn't a letter, just sort of like a letter, it didn't start with anything like Skaros Rock or Santorini, Greece. It didn't mention Skaros or Santorini or Greece at all. It only mentioned the sounds, sights, and the experience of that particular moment in 1967. And it certainly did not mention any of the harrowing experiences over the next two weeks when I was afraid I may not live to leave Greece because of the Papadopoulos coup d'état that happened the next day.

With no inkling of what lay ahead, I stuck the letter in my pocket that beautiful afternoon. And two harrowing weeks later, when I finally was able to catch a plane home to Chicago, the letter was still in my pocket. It ended up in a box in my lingerie drawer. A personal memento of survival.

Over the following decades and the next two dozen moves, the letter went with me, carefully stuffed in my box of writings and remembrances. Mementos of key moments in my life that grew as the years passed.

And then, in the spring of 2052, my great-granddaughter is cleaning out my apartment in Marseilles, France and she finds and opens the box. She has no idea of the places I traveled in my lifetime. To her, I'm an American ex-pat who spent most of my life in America and settled in France late in life. I'm long gone so she can't ask me about the letter. All she has is my recording of a moment on a piece of paper. But of everything in the box, she is drawn to this particular letter. The exact date it was written is clear—20 April of 1967. She knows I wrote it because she sees my name and my signature and it was in my box. My box in France. She reads it with great interest, having no knowledge that I spent time in Greece and having no idea what happened in Greece the day after that letter was written. She has no clue where the cliff was. And she has no idea what memories that letter held for me or what terrifying times it accompanied me through. The date of the recording is plain. Where she found the recording is clear. She sees a stain on the letter, but she has no idea it is blood or why it is there. Where the cliff and the sea were, whether it was the first time I had ever seen them. Or the people I watched die the next day. None of that can she read in the words. She has no clue of the true significance of that piece of faded paper to *me*.

Much of our most ancient recorded history is just like that letter.

We see fragments.

But time is long. And human experience is difficult to nail down in a recording.

Constellations of Stars

Think what it would have been like to be one of the earliest humans on Earth at night.

No roof above your head. Unless you were fortunate enough to find a cave unoccupied by scorpions, snakes, and bears.

Outdoors. No light other than the moon. No electricity or gas or candles or a flashlight. No fire.

Really dark. Particularly near a new moon when the moon's light was scant. Really, really dark.

And yet, there above your head were these beautiful tiny twinkling lights.

Mankind has had a fascination for the stars from the earliest days of existence on Earth. Or, from the earliest days on whatever planet man may have been on.

The stars have caught our attention and excited our imagination from the earliest beginnings of time.

About 6,500 stars are "naked-eye" stars, visible to human eyes with no type of magnification. Roughly half of those are visible at any one time from the Northern Hemisphere. The other half are visible from the Southern Hemisphere.

What exactly are constellations?

Although we do not know exactly when, from the earliest time mankind has lived on the Earth, stars have been envisioned as groups. The groups have been somewhat different from culture to culture, but putting stars in groups has been a constant across cultures.

Today we call those groupings of stars constellations.

At least that is what we call them in the West. In the East, stars were grouped differently—into what are called lunar mansions.

Besides the cultural differences, constellations are grouped by movement of the Sun. And lunar mansions are grouped by the movement of the Moon.

So since this book focuses on the Western Zodiac, lunar mansions will be mentioned in the context of being "constellations" of stars even though they are a special kind of constellation, but we will focus on the more westerly solar-based constellations. It is these solar-based constellations that are the basis of what we know as the Zodiac.

Ample record exists from Greek and Roman times about constellations, but except for scattered fragments, the majority of what we know about the constellation groupings of civilizations that pre-date ancient Greece is what the Greeks told us. Most primary records from the really, really ancient civilizations have long been lost.

And although the ancient Greeks wrote about star maps and the groupings of stars in records we have access to today, they had access to an abundance of far more ancient records from Egypt and Babylonia. We have access to those most ancient records only through the writings of the Greeks.

Diverse peoples as far afield as Australian Aboriginals, American Indians, seafaring Polynesians, Chinese, Babylonians, South Americans, and the ancient cultures of India all had divisions and recordings of stars. Despite what we may think from much of the "history" we have in the West today, the Greeks and the Romans did not have exclusive knowledge of the stars. And they certainly did not have exclusive curiosity about them.

Nonetheless, modern Western astrology is largely based on the more westerly concepts of stars and constellations that originally arose in the Middle East. Because of that, you will find this book largely focused on those origins and their evolution. And, it turns out, Western astrology is based on the most ancient of star records on Earth.

When were stars first assembled as constellations?

We aren't sure.

But let's put them in a contextual time line based on dates we do know with a degree of certainty.

The first recordings of a constellation may have been as long as 17,300 years ago.

Markings inside one of a series of 37 caves in southwestern France at Lascaux have been identified by archaeologists as possible depictions of the Pleiades star cluster and the nearby Hyades cluster. Although it is impossible to know why the people in this area in the Dordogne Valley painted star clusters on the walls and ceilings of caves or if the people who painted them knew they were stars, we can reliably date the earliest paintings in the Lascaux caves to 17,300 years ago. The vast majority of the 600 paintings at Lascaux are of animals, which make the contrasting star patterns that much more head-scratching.

The first verified records of constellations were in the long-vanished civilizations of Sumeria and Akkadia in the Middle East nearly 6,000 years ago.

Sumerian and **Akkadian** star maps from more than 5,500 years ago were incorporated into the star charts and mythology of the succeeding civilizations in the area of the world between the Tigris and the Euphrates rivers, in what is now southern Iraq. The Sumerian civilization was overtaken by neighboring Akkadia about 3,800 years ago and the resulting civilization that grew out of the merging of those two cultures we know as **Babylonia** (sometimes called by the Greek word indicating the land between the Tigris and the Euphrates, *Mesopotamia*).

By 3,000 years ago, the Babylonians had identified and were using star maps of **more than 60 constellations**. We have records of these constellations, although only from tertiary sources for the most part. We know, however, that they included Orion and (at least roughly) the constellations we today call Taurus, Leo, and Scorpio. And we also know the ancient Greeks later usurped the knowledge from these records when they conquered Babylonia.

A separate, but overlapping civilization in time to Babylonia, was **Egypt**.

Stars in Egypt were categorized in somewhat different groupings of **38 constellations**. We know they included Ursa Major ("The Great Bear") and Orion as far back as 3,100 years ago.

But the oldest known Egyptian star map, though strangely similar in some ways, was very different than the Babylonian star maps.

The earliest known Egyptian star map contains familiar constellations drawn as a Bull, a Lion, and an Eagle. But all three of them are depicted in what seems to us today to be very strange parts of the sky. The Bull is not in Taurus. The Lion is not in Leo. And the Eagle is not in Scorpio. And these earliest Egyptian constellations included both a constellation of a Man and two constellations of Crocodiles.

The most ancient Egyptian concepts of constellations appear to be more artistic than star-based because the outlines have very few actual stars in them. For example, the constellation of the Man has only one star— that appears pretty much located at the center of his stomach.

Don't confuse this very early Egyptian star map with one now located in the Louvre in Paris. The next major artifact of Egyptian constellations, called the Denderah Zodiac, was created as a bas-relief in a temple dedicated to Osiris about 3,000 years later. It has been dated to around 50 B.C.

The Denderah shows a far different zodiac that far more closely mirrors both the ancient Babylonian and Greek star maps. By the time it was constructed, almost 300 years had passed since Alexander the Great conquered Egypt and Babylonia. After three centuries of Greek dominance, Egypt clearly had lost a great deal of its original concept of the universe as it blended with the Babylonian and Greek cultures.

And for some reason, it appears the Greeks infused their science far more strongly with Babylonian science than it did with Egyptian science. But more on that later.

Star chart and constellations in the Far East about 2,500 years ago.

In China, the grouping of stars dates back to about the 500 B.C., or about 2,500 years ago. The Chinese grouped stars into what they called lunar mansions made up of 28 constellations. Unlike the Sumerians and Akkadians farther to the west who based their star groupings on the ecliptic plane of the Sun, the Chinese constellations are based on the apparent path of the Moon along the ecliptic plane rather than of the Sun.

But the Chinese awareness of constellations was not static. By about 150 B.C., the Chinese recognized nearly 90 constellations. And by 400 A.D., the Chinese were using star maps of 284 constellations!

Probably largely because they are based on the apparent path of the Moon rather than of the Sun, these Chinese constellations look nothing like the star maps of constellations that developed in the West. The most ancient Chinese star map centered on the celestial north poles of 1,460 stars. And unlike more westerly peoples, the Chinese grouped stars into much smaller "constellations." Likewise, Chinese mythology surrounding most of these star groupings is very different from Western mythology.

The use of the Chinese constellations, or lunar mansions, spread across Japan, Korea, and most of south-east Asia. The lunar mansion star map is still widely used in China today, often side-by-side with the modern Western constellation map.

About the same distance in the past—about the 5th Century B.C. or 2,500 years ago—there is evidence that there were both star catalogs and categorical groupings of stars in use in India. Exactly how far back this stretches before that time is uncertain. Indian astrology, typically called Hindi astrology or Vedic astrology, recognizes 27 groups of stars termed nakastras. As you might guess given the length of time it has been used in India, a large body of Vedic mythology exists about these 27 nakastras.

The ancient Greek constellations from about 2,300 years ago.

The legendary Greek ruler Alexander the Great conquered Egypt in 332 B.C. and then his army moved on over to conquer the ancient civilization of Babylonia in 331 B.C. That was more than 300 years before the birth of Jesus of Nazareth.

We need to keep in mind here that both Egypt and Babylonia were very old civilizations when Alexander captured them. And both had long-developed science and cosmology.

While we have archaeological evidence of a civilization in Egypt dating as far back as 6,000 years before the birth of Jesus, the first Dynasty of Egypt dates to 3414 B.C.

Keep in mind that as of the date of the writing of this book, the 1st Dynasty of Egypt was almost five-and-a-half thousand years ago. Not 550. But 5,500.

Babylon is a little more recent, but the first Dynasty of Babylon dates to 1894 B.C.— almost four thousand years ago. But remember, Babylonian was essentially an evolution of the merging of the even more ancient neighboring cultures of Sumeria and Akkadia that stretch back, with both science and astronomy, to almost 6,000 years ago.

In a world that lives and breathes on
Instagram and Snapchat,
it is difficult to wrap our brains
around the length of this kind of time.

But for the purposes of understanding how the concept of constellations developed, it is inherently part of the understanding.

We have no books from the ancient Egyptian and Babylonian civilizations about constellations or about the details of their observations or their science or their beliefs. But we do have records of what the Greeks said about the recorded knowledge and science of Egypt and Babylonia in the years following Greek supremacy of the prior cultures.

Because of these takeovers by ancient Greece about 330 years before the birth of Jesus, all of the knowledge and science and wisdom of way-way-ancient Egypt and way-ancient Babylonia were incorporated into ancient Greek knowledge. And we can read what some of the greatest Greek minds wrote about the records they had.

So we have information dating back, or at least possibly dating back, almost 6,000 years. It just comes from a second-hand source.

Second-hand knowledge and Star Catalogs from early Ancient Greece.

About two hundred years before the birth of Jesus of Nazareth, a man we simply know today as **Hipparchus** (190 B.C-120 B.C.) was born in Nicea—an area in what had been and is today Egypt, but that had been overtaken by Greece about 140 years earlier. Hipparchus was born a Greek citizen. And from the records we have, he was an exceptionally bright student who gravitated to the Greek center of learning on the island of Rhodes. He continued to study and work most of his life in Rhodes in the areas of mathematics and astronomy.

We have access to at least some of Hipparchus's writings today. And we know he wrote a lot about the records he saw firsthand from the Egyptians and Babylonians. He examined them, re-explained them, then expanded on them through his own observations and knowledge.

One of the many things Hipparchus did was to catalog 850 stars. How much of that information was based on more ancient knowledge and how much was based on his personal observations of the sky, we do not know.

27

Hipparchus also came up with a scale of star "magnitude" (or brightness). He developed another little concept we still use today called Trigonometry. He measured the distance between the Earth and the Moon (accurately by the way). He said he was certain that "fixed" stars actually weren't fixed but instead moved very, very slowly— although it took several millennia for science to accept that as true. He recorded the first observed nova. And, if that were not enough, Hipparchus was the first person to discover that the equinoxes and solstices were not fixed, but changing in sky placement, what we call today the Precession of the Equinoxes.

Unfortunately we no longer have the catalog of stars Hipparchus came up with from his observations. But 300 years after Hipparchus, another scientist who did have access to those records, used them and expanded on them.

Third-hand knowledge and Constellation Maps from later Ancient Greece.

Three hundred years after Hipparchus lived and worked, another Greek mathematician and astronomer studied Hipparchus's work in the Great Library in Alexandria.

Claudius Ptolemy (85 A.D.-165 A.D.), also a Greek citizen born in the land of ancient Egypt, was a scholar who spent most of his working life at the legendary Great Library in Alexandria.

Keep in mind that after Greece conquered Egypt and Babylon and most of every inch of land in the Mediterranean World as well as large portions of southern and central Asia and India, the vast majority of the ancient knowledge and science of the world was gathered together in the Greek library in Alexandria.

And although Alexandria, or what is left today of ancient Alexandria, is located in what has re-become the country of Egypt, during Ptolemy's lifetime, as during Hipparchus's lifetime, it was part of Greece. And by the time Ptolemy was born, all of the ancient world's greatest scholars and scientists gathered in Alexandria to study at this amazing library. It literally contained the history and knowledge of the world.

Ptolemy was quite prolific. In fact, among his writings was a 13-book treatise originally titled *The Mathematical Compilation* (in Greek, of course). Fortunately that treatise was considered so monumental that it was translated from the original Greek into Arabic. The Arabs translated the name for Ptolemy's treatise to the Arabic word *Almagest* and spread copies of it across the

Arabic world for study, which meant that it was still in existence after the Great Library was destroyed. The Arabic translation of Ptolemy's 13-book treatise later was translated from Arabic into Latin, then from Latin into almost every known language. The name we call that book today is still *Almagest*, from the Arabic translation that saved it for the world.

Ptolemy's book *Almagest* and Euclid's book *Elements* (as it is known in English) are the two longest-used scientific books on the planet.

In *Almagest*, Ptolemy took the works of Hipparchus and expanded on them with his own study of other records and his own observation of the heavens. He created one of the first groupings of stars into "constellations" that we have existing record of. And it is that grouping of constellations upon which our modern set of constellations is based.

The 48 "Classical Constellations" from Ptolemy about 1,900 years ago.

In one of the books of the *Almagest*, written about 150 A.D., Ptolemy cataloged 1,028 celestial objects. Most of the objects listed are stars that Ptolemy categorized into the **48 constellations** we now call the "**Classical Constellations**."

It bears noting that Ptolemy listed three stars *twice* in his catalog.

No, it was not a mistake. Ptolemy considered three specific stars more important than the rest because he envisioned each of these stars as "belonging" to more than one constellation. The three stars he listed as being shared by two constellations are Formalhaut, Beta Tauri, and Nu Boötes.

FORMALHAUT.

The star **Formalhaut** Ptolemy describes as the end of the flow of water from the urn in **Aquarius** and also as the star at the mouth of the constellation of **Piscis Austrinus**.

For those not die-hard sky-watchers, the name Piscis Austrinus is unfamiliar. But in both the Classical and the Modern Constellations, Piscis Austrinus is called "The Great Fish" that parented the two smaller fish that make up the more familiar constellation of Pisces.

So Formalhaut is listed twice by Ptolemy, but only one of the mentions falls in a sign of our modern zodiac.

BETA TAURI.

The star **Beta Tauri** is described by Ptolemy as the tip of the northern horn of **Taurus** and also as the right ankle of the constellation of **Auriga**.

And again, most readers have probably not heard of the constellation Auriga "The Charioteer."

So like Formalhaut, Beta Tauri falls in only one of our modern zodiac constellations: Taurus.

NU BOÖTES.

The star **Nu Boötes** is shown in Ptolemy's catalog on the right foot of the constellation of **Hercules** and also at the top of the staff of the constellation of **Boötes**.

You have probably heard of Hercules, though you may not associate it with a constellation in the sky. But actually the constellation of Hercules takes up a lot of celestial real estate. In fact, it is the 5th largest of the modern constellations. But despite its size, even the ancient Greeks had lost its more ancient meaning. Taken from the Babylonian star charts, a great deal of mythology grew up around Hercules, yet much of it is conflicting. And, at least as far as we know, Hercules is surrounded by a lot of mythology, but it never was considered part of the Zodiac as we think of a zodiac.

The constellation of Boötes (pronounced Boh-oh-tease) is positioned directly behind the "The Great Bear" (Ursa Major). It's name literally means the "bear keeper," but it is usually referred to today as "The Herdsman."

Neither of Ptolemy's mentions of Nu Boötes falls in a modern zodiac constellation.

Ptolemy's catalog of constellations was revised by the Persian astronomer Abd al-Rahmān al-Sūfī in the 10th Century A.D., then expanded greatly by the Danish astronomer Tycho Brahe in the 16th century. But the base Ptolemy laid tracing back to the earliest Babylonian star maps remains indelibly marked in our concepts of constellations.

The 88 "Modern Constellations"

Up until the 16th Century A.D., all of the star maps and constellation catalogs we know of contained stars only in the Northern Hemisphere or barely over the edge of the equator into the Southern Hemisphere.

As far as we know, the great ancient civilizations of the Northern Hemisphere had not yet begun to venture much below the equator. And the great civilizations of the Southern Hemisphere had not ventured above the equator. We lived in a very separated world that makes our modern East/West divisions seem both porous and pretty much invisible. The equator, however, seemed to be a far more impenetrable barrier for some reason.

Then, between the 16th and 17th centuries A.D., we saw the Great Age of Exploration. Shipbuilding and sailing reached heights of achievement unparalleled in history. And through a series of great navigators and explorers, European exploration of the planet mushroomed. For the first time, at least in recorded history, the Southern Hemisphere was widely explored by peoples from the Northern Hemisphere. And along with it, the skies of the Southern Hemisphere were both seen and mapped.

Consequently, star knowledge increased exponentially. And gradually, so did the expansion of groupings of stars into "new" constellations. Of course, these stars were not new, but they were indeed new to star maps.

The first major overhaul of Ptolemy's star map was made by Danish astronomer Tycho Brahe (1546–1601 A.D.). But he was far from the only one who expanded the star map over the next several centuries. Each exploration seemed to add more. But Tycho Brahe's changes were the most sweeping and mathematically accurate. And they incorporated a huge volume of new information that seemed to be continually added to over the next several centuries.

By the 20th Century A.D., the amount of new celestial knowledge was astronomical. (Pardon the pun.) And modern astronomers decided we needed to have a comprehensive and clear map of the heavens. In the mid-1920s, the International Astronomical Union (the "IAU") commissioned the French draftsman Eugene Delaporte (1882-1953 A.D.) to draw a new all-encompassing star map of constellations with definite boundaries between the constellations. So at the behest of the IAU, in 1930 Delaport published a revolutionary new constellation map *Délimitation scientifique des constellations,* or in English, *The Scientific Demarcation of the Constellations.*

Not only did Delaport's new map include the Southern Hemisphere, but instead of the locational boundaries between constellations being designated as "the foot" or "the end of the flow of water" or "the tip of the northern horn," in this new map, the dividing lines between constellations were altered to be clear, distinct, and certain boundaries. And for the first time, possibly in history, all countries began using the same astronomical map.

But even more significantly, the "official" number of constellations in the sky, including stars in the Southern Hemisphere as well as the Northern Hemisphere along with a number of newly-found variable stars, went from 48 to 88.

Lest one think there was a simple addition of 40 constellations, that was not exactly true. Several "boundary" lines were re-drawn and at least one constellation was defrocked of its "constellation-ness." Although I have been able to locate no written reason, Delaport summarily removed the constellation **Antinous** from the constellation map. Antinous had been deigned a constellation in 132 A.D. by the Roman Emperor Hadrian and had survived numerous constellation "re-writes." It turns out poor Antinous was just as mysterious as a constellation as his death was in the 2nd Century. And perhaps just as controversial.

I mention Antinous here not to get us off track, but to highlight two things.

One, what constitutes "boundary" lines in the sky are changeable no matter how fixed a man or a culture wants them to be.

And two, modern mores and religious-leanings are integrally intertwined with how we view the heavens. The story of Antinous, a real human in recorded history, by the way, would shock the conscience of most modern people. And it is at least remotely possible that the moral repugnance of Antinous's life is the reason his constellation was ripped from the sky in the 1920s. That change in constellations may well have had more to do with morality of the times and judgment about morality of the past than with science.

We will find other examples of these kinds of changes as we explore each Zodiac constellation   one-by-one.

If there are 88 Constellations, why twelve Zodiac Signs?

S ome people seem to think that the only constellations in the sky are the twelve signs of the Zodiac. But that clearly is not the case.

The twelve "signs" of the Zodiac are indeed all constellations. But they are a very special grouping of constellations.

Constellations are grouped by things like the Animal Constellations or the Dog Constellations or the Water Constellations or the Fish Constellations. Of course, several overlap.

But the constellations that seem to have remained most special over the history of mankind are the ones we call the Zodiac Constellations. And it may surprise you to learn there are actually thirteen Zodiac Constellations, not just twelve.

At least there are today.

But if we look far enough back in history, twelve was not always some kind of "magic number."

In the oldest Babylonian zodiac, which the Babylonians took at least in part from the older Sumerians, there were as many as eighteen Zodiac Constellations and all eighteen signs were used in their astrology. Over the centuries, the Babylonians shrank their zodiac down to twelve signs.

But we will get to that in due time.

For now, what makes a constellation a Zodiac Constellation?

Today our definition of a Zodiac Constellation is scientific. Well, at least pretty much scientific.

Here's how a "Zodiac" constellation is determined by astronomers.

We all know that the Sun is a fixed star that moves, but barely moves. And we know the Earth consistently rotates on its axis about every 24 hours. That's why we have day—when our half of the Earth is "facing" the Sun. And that's why we have night—when our half of the Earth is "facing away from" the Sun.

The "path" of the Sun is similar as it "moves" through the sky over the course of a year.

What astronomers call the **ecliptic** is an imaginary line in the sky that marks the annual path of the Sun. It is the projection of Earth's orbit onto the celestial sphere. And from our most ancient times, this annual path of the Sun has been used to mark seasons of the year.

The Zodiac Constellations are those special constellations that lie along the ecliptic plane—right in line with the apparent annual movement of the Sun through our sky.

The Sun "moves" through the Zodiac Constellations and the rest of the constellations, the Sun never appears in.

But here is the thing about the Zodiac Constellations that really surprises most people. There actually are thirteen of them.

Ever hear of **Ophiuchus**? Probably not. Don't worry. You are in good company. Most people haven't.

Ophiuchus ("oh-fee-YEW-kuss") is a constellation called "The Serpent Bearer." It lies along the ecliptic in the natural Zodiac zone right between Sagittarius and Scorpio. In fact, it "robs" a section of each constellation. But I'm pretty certain you have never seen it in a chart. And more than likely this is the first time you have heard the word.

A few, a very few, astrologers use Ophiuchus in charts. And the very few who do seem to hold no consensus on its meaning or even its use in an astrological chart. In fact, most seem to use Ophiuchus much as a superimposition on the "existing" signs of Scorpio and Sagittarius, much like they read extra meaning of a fixed star in a sector of a chart.

Lots of conjecture exists as to why, since there are actually thirteen constellations along the ecliptic, astrologers all the way back to Babylonian times have held the Zodiac to twelve constellations and have ignored the thirteenth.

But remaining true to what we actually see in the heavens, whatever reason the thirteenth sign has been omitted from the astrological wheel, there actually are thirteen constellations that meet the astronomical definition of Zodiac Constellations.

Changes from the

original Zodiac

symbols.

When we talk about the word "symbol" in this book, we are talking about the **conceptual** symbol attached to a Zodiac constellation, or to what astrologers call a "Zodiac sign." This conceptual symbol is distinct from the **glyph** symbol that is used for a Zodiac sign. Although a glyph is indeed a symbol of sorts, in the language of astrology the glyphs function more as an alphabet than as conceptual symbolic depictions.

Here is an example.

CONCEPTUAL symbols.

The Zodiac constellation of Gemini, or the astrological sign of Gemini, is characterized conceptually as "The Twins." Over millennia artists have drawn, painted, and sculpted works of art showing the twins. The **conceptual symbol** of Gemini is twins. Sometimes this concept has been depicted as a marble sculpture of two identical males standing side-by-side, sometimes as a painting of two females seated facing each other, sometimes a metal etching of a twin of each gender with their backs to each other, sometimes the twins are mirror images holding hands, sometimes only the faces are shown of almost identical twins with one who has curly hair and who has straight hair. All sorts of different ideas and shades of human twins arise out of the *conceptual symbol* of Gemini.

GLYPH symbols.

And yet, when an astrological chart is drafted, there is a symbol used for Gemini in the chart. That symbol is called a glyph.

The glyph symbol for Gemini is c.

The glyph also is conceptual in a manner, but it carries a different and a deeper meaning than simply the concept of Gemini as twins. And, unlike the conceptual symbol, that one glyph is used repeatedly across time and cultures. It may vary to the extent that human hand-writing varies, but the glyph is repeated as exactly as the accuracy of the human hand allows.

Although a glyph is indeed a symbol, it is more than a symbol. A glyph is concise and stylized. And it functions as a part of a very special alphabet more similar in its richness of meaning to Chinese characters or Vedic symbols than to what we consider the ABCs of the Western alphabet.

Glyphs are not part of what this book explores. The glyphs are deeply explored in the four-part series *Reading by Symbol Light: Astrology in its Native Language.* But in this book we are looking solely at the **conceptual** symbols of astrology that show up in mythology.

So when you read the word "symbol" in this book, understand it is the conceptual symbol that is being explored, not the glyph.

The most dramatic changes in Zodiac symbolism are the types of beings associated with the signs.

In our most ancient Earth history and in most of the Earth's mythology, people envisioned beings unlike anything in our world. Myth is filled with unnatural or supernatural beings—or at the very least with beings we have no concept of today except though reading mythologies from the Earth's distant past.

The oldest accounts of Zodiac constellations and Zodiac signs include them even though most of them have more or less vanished from our modern Zodiac.

Most of these strange beings are animal "hybrids" that seem like science fiction to us today. Some are even animal/human hybrids. You will read about some of them as we sift through the history of constellation mythology and Zodiac symbolism. But, in general, there are a few groups of these surreal beings it is important to understand.

ANIMAL HYBRIDS.

There are quadrupeds with bird wings— such as the winged horse Pegasus, the winged deer Peyton, winged cats, winged lions, winged unicorns (called *alicorns*).

There are three-headed serpents such as Cerberus. There are Kelpies who are half horse and half fish. There is the Griffin with the front quarters of an eagle and the hind quarters of a lion that was used even in

46

modern times on the national insignia of Prussia.

These fantastical creatures exist in cultures worldwide.

In Egypt there was the Criosphinx with the body of a lion and the head of a ram. In Babylonia there was the Serpopard with its mixed snake, dinosaur, and African leopard body. In India there was Gajmina who had the body of a fish and the head of an elephant. In Persia there was the Simurgh with its dog head, lion claws, and griffin-like body. In China there was the Gye-long a creature with the head of a chicken and the body of a dragon. In Japan there was the Nue with the head of a monkey, the legs of a tiger, the body of a raccoon, and the front-half of a snake for a tail. And in the Mesoamericas there were the Kukulkan and Quetzalcoatl that were feathered serpents with wings.

Some were very specific to astrology, such as the Sea-Goat of Capricornius—a being half fish and half goat with very rich ancient legend.

ANIMAL-HUMAN HYBRIDS.

The most familiar animal-human hybrid to most people is a Centaur—a creature with the upper body of a human and the lower body of a horse. Today we think of them as benign.

But they weren't. To the ancients they symbolized barbarism and unbridled chaos.

There actually are a lot of varieties of Centaurs or Centaur-like creatures. Like Satyrs. The original Greek Satyrs were particularly nasty creatures prone to violence, drunkenness, and sexual depravity. Satyrs had human bodies with the pointed ears and the long tail of a horse. Over the centuries Satyrs grew to be more often depicted as men with the horns and legs of a goat, much like the Roman creature the Faun. Although the Roman Faun creature had a very different personality and character than the Satyr.

Some of these creatures were humans that were mixed not only with a horse or a goat, but with a donkey, a bird, a fish, a snake, a turtle, a scorpion, a lion, or even a dog. Some were a mixture of two, some three, some as many as five different species.

And some of these animal-human hybrids were associated with ancient astrology.

For example, the Ichthyocentaurs ("ik thee oh sin tors") were a race with the torso of a man or woman, the front legs of a horse, and the tail of a fish. Even though it is long-forgotten in modern astrological symbolism, an Ichthyocentaur is embedded in the most ancient legends of the signs of both Cancer and Pisces.

Fantastical and supernatural beings—or possibly long extinct beings—are inherently part of Earth's mythology. And they are more deeply a part of astrology than we remember.

Space Exploration in

the 21st Century

Ｔhe 16th and 17th Centuries are considered The Great Age of Exploration—of the Earth. This planet.

But history will doubtlessly look at the 20th and 21st Centuries as another great age of exploration. This time the exploration is not focused on our own planet as much as it is fixed on the space outside of and beyond Earth.

In the mid-20th Century, mankind first launched a human into "space," that area beyond the atmosphere of the Earth. And in less than a decade man flew to the Earth's Moon.

In the years following man's first lunar landing in 1969, we have seen a virtual tidal wave of new kinds of telescopes and rockets and satellites and space probes. And although many of these innovations have lost the prominence in the public eye that landing a man on the moon had, over the past century, we have explored deeper and deeper into space with increasingly sophisticated probes. And our body of our scientific knowledge has increased exponentially because of it.

Both our ability to see from the earth in terms of telescope technologies, and our ability to actually get to other constellations, stars, and planets in terms of spacecraft have mushroomed.

In fact, since 2000 A.D., seventeen nations have banded together to maintain and continually man a permanent research facility in outer space that we call a "space station." Only a few decades earlier, our space station would have been considered science fiction, not real science.

We have sent un-manned space probes in multiple different forms to virtually every constellation. Some have continually been sending data about space back to earth for several decades. Many go "online" with new data coming back yearly, sometimes monthly. Some of these information-gathering spaceships have no chance of giving us data during our lifetimes. And even if everything on the journey goes well, at least one will not make it to its destination for two million years.

The short road from exploration to colonization.

The United States National Aeronautics and Space Administration ("NASA") landed an unmanned robot on Mars in August of 2012 named **Curiosity**. As of the date of this book's publication, Curiosity is still roving the planet of Mars gathering and sending information to Earth.

And based largely on what we have learned from Curiosity, NASA has another launch planned for July 2020 of an unmanned craft to land on Mars for even more sophisticated exploration. That mission is designed to test a method for producing sufficient oxygen from the Martian atmosphere for a human to live on Mars in a self-sustaining manner. It also is planned to test techniques for improved landings on Mars, to identify other resources on Mars such as the availability of subsurface water, and to gather more-specific information about surface dust, weather patterns and potential environmental conditions that would affect humans living and working on Mars. And, since we are curious beings, part of that mission is to gather more information about past microbial life on Mars.

That launch, **Mars Rover 2020**, is set for slightly more than a year from the writing of this book.

We clearly live in a time that the lines between fiction and reality are blurring.

But the next phases of the Mars Rover mission is considerably more historic.

In 2030, NASA plans to land humans on Mars in order to establish a space station on the surface of Mars—potentially to pave the way for colonization.

Science fiction becomes less fictional every day.

Zodiac Constellations

Reconsidered, Again

Fiction is about imaginary people, places,
and things, not "real" ones.

Think about that a minute.

Less than 100 years ago if you read that a
man had walked on the moon, that men were
living on a ship in the sky, or that we were
actively planning to colonize Mars, you would
have unquestioningly said it was fiction. Not
reality. Imaginary people doing imaginary
things in imaginary places. Fiction. Not
reality.

The line between them is thinner than we
think.

What if that line between fiction and reality extends to the past as well as to the future?

A child was born seven years ago in a remote village in an under-developed country in a dwelling with a dirt floor, no running water, no indoor toilet, no electricity, no television, no books, parents who can neither read nor write, and virtually no access to a larger world outside of her rural community. As fictional as that may sound to us, there are many places and people like that on this planet right now in this moment in time. To her, is toilet paper fictional? How about GPS or Snapchat? Or equal rights for women?

In looking back at the ancient mythology of constellations, it may be worth keeping those questions in mind.

THE

CONSTELLATION OF

ARIES

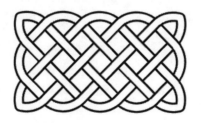

How Aries was seen in

antiquity.

In the most ancient of Earth's history, the star patterns in or near the modern constellation of Aries took on different symbolism in different cultures. In some of the earliest cultures in the Indus Valley, it was seen as a farmhand. In China, it was seen as the twin inspectors. And in the Marshall Islands, it was seen as a porpoise or dolphin.

But evidence suggests that Aries has been represented by a Ram, or at least a type of Ram-like being, since at least late Babylonian times, at least as far back as 2000 B.C. On early clay tablets in Babylonia, Aries is described as the final station along the ecliptic.

The earliest accounts we have today of Aries as a distinct constellation come from boundary stones that date back between 1350 B.C. and 1000 BC. The zodiac depiction of a Ram figure is distinct from the other characters present on several of the stones. This dates a shift in identification from the constellation Aries as the agrarian worker to identification with the Ram. Most antiquarians agree the shift likely occurred much earlier, but is only recorded later in Babylonian records. The exact timing of the shift is difficult to determine due to the lack of images of Aries or other Ram-like figures

In ancient Egyptian astronomy, Aries was associated with the God **Amon-Ra**, who is depicted as a type of Centaur—one that is **half man and half goat**, but in a reverse combination of how most Centaurs are represented. In the antiquities of Egypt this half-man/half-goat god was shown as a man with the head of a ram. This odd Goat Centaur Amon- Ra represented fertility and creativity in ancient Egypt.

The constellation of Aries was located on the vernal equinox at the time—a time before the Earth wobbled out of that trajectory, back when the Tropical Zodiac was the Zodiac seen in the sky.

Because of the eventual precession of equinoxes, Aries began to be called the "Indicator of the Reborn Sun."

During the times of the year when Aries was prominent, priests would erect statues of

Amon-Ra in temples, a practice continued in a modified form by Persian astronomers centuries later. Aries became known as "Lord of the Head" during this time in Egypt. But Aries was not yet considered a constellation.

In the astrology of ancient Greece, the constellation of Aries is associated with the Golden Ram or the Golden Fleece of Greek mythology. That ram was envisioned as **a four-legged creature with wing**s and **golden wool**. But it also was associated with **Ares**, the Greek god of War. The *male* god of war, who was conceived as very different from the *female* god of War Athena.

To the Greeks, Ares represented the **gory**, **violent**, and **untamed** aspects of wars, not the strategic, intelligent, well-planned aspects of war that were left to the domain of Athena.

As one modern historian has described it, Ares was Rambo and Athena was Napoleon.

These two Greek war gods give deep insight to the constellation, but also to how the Greeks viewed war.

And then, as the Romans did with almost all of Greek mythology, Ares was renamed **Mars** and the legend and the characteristics were changed ever-so-slightly.

When the Greek astronomer-astrologer Ptolemy created a catalog of constellations in the 2nd Century B.C., he did not categorize Aries as a constellation. Instead, he labeled it an "unformed star," and specifically the "Star Over the Head."

Since the symbolic shift from **Farm Worker** to Ram, Aries has been associated in astrology with the head and all things related to the head and face.

But we know from the distinction between Ares and Athena, that the ancient Greeks saw Aries more represented by **ramming with the head** than **using** the head.

Since Greek times, the sign of Aries has been considered to govern **Western Europe** and **Syria** in mundane astrology. And in natal and horary astrology, Aries has indicated a person with a **strong temper and short fuse**.

Medieval Arabian astrologers depicted Aries in several ways, with lack of apparent consensus. Some depicted Aries in a similar manner to Ptolemy's concept of a Man-Ram. However, some Islamic celestial globes show Aries as a nondescript four-legged animal with what could be **antlers rather than horns**. We find records of early Bedouin observers noting a Ram elsewhere in the sky, not in Aries. The most widely-held ancient Arabic concept of Aries, however, consisted of 13 stars in a figure along with five "unformed" stars, four of which were over the animal's hindquarters and one of which was one of the disputed stars over Aries' head. But the famous Arabic astronomer-astrologer Al-Sufi's depiction of Aries differed. Al-Sufi saw Aries as a Ram, but as a Ram **running at full speed and looking behind itself as it ran**.

In traditional Chinese astronomy, stars from Aries were seen as parts of several different constellations. To the ancient Chinese, Aries was considered the 16th lunar mansion, the location of the full moon closest to the autumnal equinox.

In a system similar to the ancient Chinese, the first lunar mansion in Hindu astronomy was called "Aswini," named after two of the stars in what we now call the constellation of Aries.

In Hebrew astronomy, Aries was referred to as "Tel." And it represented either Simeon or Gad, symbolizing "Lamb of the World"— many centuries before Jesus of Nazareth was called by that name.

The Hebrews' neighbors, the Syrians, named the Aries constellation *Amru*. And the nearby Turks named it *Kuzi*.

On the other side of the planet, in the Marshall Islands, several stars in what we today consider Aries were envisioned as part of a constellation they called "The Porpoise" or "The Dolphin." No Ram or Man-Ram was part of their cosmology.

Then, moving closer to "modern" times, as summarized in 1653 by the London astrologer William Ramesey in his seminal work Astrologia Restaurata:

> *The first sign is called Aries (signifying a Ram,) because when the Sun is therein, he approacheth to his highest point; heat (thereby being increased, yet being mixed with the humidity of the preceding Winter, makes the fi temperature of the ayr hot and moyst, which is according to the complexion of the Ram: but there are some of the Ancients say that the stars in the signs being particularly observed, and as it were measured with a line the one from the other, they resemble each the thing they are nominated.*

What we know about the constellation of Aries today.

Aries is a mid-size constellation. It ranks 39th in size among the modern 88 constellations. Aries occupies an area of 441 square degrees in the sky. It is not very luminous and has only three stars that are considered "bright."

Although Aries was one of the 48 constellations described by 2nd century Greek astrologer Ptolemy (and was seen, known, and used by astrologers long before Ptolemy lived), Aries wasn't fully recognized by the IAU until 1922. And its boundaries as a modern constellation were not defined until 1930.

Aries is located in the northern hemisphere between the constellation of Pisces, which is to the West of Aries, and Taurus to its east. In North America, it is best viewed in the sky during the month of December around 9 PM.

Multiple stars in Aries with exoplanets.

We know today that the constellation of Aries contains several stars with known planets orbiting them. **Hamal** (Alpha Arietis), **Sheratan** (Beta Arietis), and **Mesartim** (Gamma Arietis), are the Taurus's three brightest stars.

The brightest of the three stars in Aries is **Hamal**, an orange giant star. Hamal is the Arabic word for "Lamb" or "head of the RAM." Hamal is 66 light-years from Earth and has at least one orbiting planet with the mass greater than Jupiter's.

The next brightest star in Aries is **Sheratan**, a bright blue star 59 light-years away from Earth.

And the third, **Mesartim**, is an off-white binary star, one with the magnitude of 4.59, the other with the magnitude of 4.68.

In addition to these three bright stars and the planets orbiting them, there are at least three other stars in Aries with orbiting planets.

One of the dimmer stars in Aries, HIP 14810 is orbited by three giant planets, each more than ten times the size of Earth.

Another of these dimmer stars, named HD 12661, has two planets that are both larger than Jupiter.

And another of these dimmer stars in the constellation of Aries is HD 20367. It has one known planet about the same mass as Jupiter.

Other atypical features of Aries.

The constellation of Aries has only few known significant nebulae and galaxies. But the galaxies within Aries include spiral galaxies, elliptical galaxies, and interacting galaxies. The variety is notable.

New insights into the

meaning of Aries?

Modern astrology clearly has lost the most ancient symbolism of a Centaur creature in connection with the sign of Aries.

Today we see Aries as a normal Ram.

To the ancients it was a **man-creature**. Albeit a highly valuable one. And one with great bravery.

We do, however, retain the maleness characteristics from the ancient Greeks even though it is so buried in our concept that most people may not readily make the distinction. A Ram is a sheep. But a male sheep. This likely is a holdover of the division between Ares and Athena, with a specific distinction mostly lost.

Even though Aries is associated with the head, the actual astronomy of the constellation shows it to be not very "bright."

If we combine that with the remembrance that the ancients saw Ares as a hero on the battlefield, but one who was a **"hot head"** that **"rammed"** though violently without thinking or planning, that the constellation is a dim one should give us a little bit of a chuckle.

While no specific mention is made in antiquity about Ares wearing armor, many accounts explicitly say that Athena wore amour in battle. One might deduce Ares didn't even take the time to don protection before rushing into battle.

Athena probably needed Ares' brawn.
But Ares certainly could use more of Athena's brains.

In parsing through our most ancient and our most recent information, these kinds of symbolic and poetic shadows may open our eyes to see Aries in a more nuanced way. And it may guide us to look at combativeness in ourselves and in Arian people and planets that fall in Aries a more insightful way as well.

Certainly looking at the past concepts and the physical facts we have garnered about the constellation points us to some new things to ponder about Aries—some actually quite ancient.

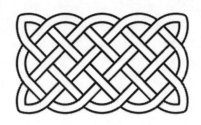

THE

CONSTELLATION OF

TAURUS

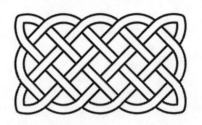

How Taurus was seen

in antiquity.

The constellation of Taurus was the first constellation in the Babylonian zodiac.

The Babylonians described Taurus as **"the bull in front"** or **"the lead bull"** or sometimes "the Bull of Heaven." Interestingly, in American cattle drives in the "old West" cowpunchers always identified the lead bull in order to move large herds of cattle.

In the earliest known star catalogs of the Babylonians, on the Spring Equinox the Sun was in Taurus. It had not yet moved to Aries.

In the old Babylonian epic of Gilgamesh, the goddess Ishtar enticed Taurus, the Bull of Heaven, to kill Gilgamesh for spurning her advances. In this skirmish the bull is pulled apart by Gilgamesh and pieces of him are hurled into the sky where, according to the legend, they became the stars we know as Ursa Major and Ursa Minor.

Many ancient cultures had bull legends. The legends differed, at least slightly. And different legends in different cultures placed the bull in different places in the sky, not always in the constellation of Taurus.

Equally intriguing as the plethora of differing bull legends in antiquity are the similarities of ancient beliefs connected to the stars in Taurus—particularly the Pleiades.

The main star cluster in Taurus, the Pleiades, has been referred to as the seven sisters in many cultures and languages across the globe, including indigenous groups in Australia, North America, and Siberia. This suggests the name had a common ancient origin. It also suggests wide travel between cultures in the Earths distant past.

In early Babylonian art, the **Bull of Heaven** was closely associated with Inanna, the Samarian goddess of **sexual love**, **fertility**, and **warfare**. One of the oldest Babylonian depictions shows the bull standing before the goddess.

The same iconic representation of the heavenly bull was reflected in Egyptian bas-relief.

In both the ancient Babylonian and ancient Egyptian cultures, the orientation of the horns was portrayed as upward or backward. The direction of the horns differ from the later Greek depiction of the horns pointing forward.

To the Egyptians, the bull in the constellation of Taurus was sacred and closely associated with the **renewal of life** and **spring**. When the spring equinox entered Taurus, the constellation would become covered by the sun in the western sky. To them, this was an obvious sign of the beginning of spring.

To the early Hebrews, Taurus also was the first constellation in their zodiac. Consequently, Taurus is represented by the first letter in the Hebrew alphabet, Aleph.

In Greek mythology, Taurus was identified with Zeus, who assumed the form of a **magnificent white bull** on more than one occasion. He often took this form to charm beautiful young maidens and lure them away with him. His jealous wife Hera had ample reason to be jealous. Zeus was constantly seducing young virgins and trying to hide the fact from his wife Hera.

Some historians say that Taurus is the formation of the myth of the Cretan bull, one of the Twelve Labors of Heracles (later appearing as the Roman myth about Hercules).

In a totally different part of the world, Taurus became an important object of worship among the Druids, the ancient learned ones of the Celts.

Among the Arctic peoples known as the Inuit, the symbolism of Taurus is not so much a bull as it is a **polar bear**. To the Inuit, the bright red star of *Aldebaran* represents the bear. The remainder of the star cluster in the Hyades is seen as a pack of dogs holding the beast at bay.

In Buddhism, legends hold that the good Bhutto was born when the full moon was in Vaisajha, or Taurus. Buddha's birthday is celebrated with a festival that occurs on the first or second full moon when the Sun is in Taurus.

And in the words of Western astrologer William Ramesey in 1653 in *Astrologia Restaurata* (London):

> *The second sign is called Taurus (signifying a Bull) because the Sun being therein, the heat is more fixt and fortified, and the moisture consumed or expelled; the temperature of the ayr tending rather to dryness, which resembleth the nature of a Bull.*

What we know about the constellation of Taurus today.

The identification of the constellation of Taurus with the bull is very old. It dates back to the Chalcolithic, and perhaps even to the upper Paleolithic periods of Earth's pre-history. Researchers at the University of Munich believe that Taurus is represented in a cave painting at the Hall of the Bulls in the caves at Lascaux, France (dated to roughly 15,000 BC).

Taurus is one of the most noticeable constellations as well as one of the oldest documented constellations.

Taurus is famous for its giant red star, Aldebaran, as well as a star cluster known as the Pleiades, sometimes called "The Seven Sisters."

The name **Aldebaran** comes from the Arabic word meaning "The Follower" because it appears to follow the Hyades star cluster that forms the head of the bull.

Aldebaran is the brightest star in the constellation and the fourteenth brightest star in the entire sky. It is a red star, considered an orange-hued red, approximately 65 light-years from Earth. It forms part of a V-shaped group of stars called The Hyades that usually are seen as a bull's face. Aldebaran is often depicted as glaring at Orion "the Hunter" situated in a constellation just to the southwest of Aldebaran.

The Earth space probe Pioneer 10 is currently moving in the general direction of Aldebaran and is expected to make its closest pass by the star in roughly 2 million years, according to NASA. Clearly, Aldebaran is a long, long way away from Earth.

The other major star in Taurus is actually a star cluster called the **Pleiades**, or **"The Seven Sisters."** This cluster consists of seven stars that appear to be resting on the bull's shoulder. According to NASA data released in 2017, six of the seven stars in this cluster are variable B stars that change brightness over the course of one day.

Although the number of visible stars in the Pleiades varies depending on local atmospheric conditions and an individual's eyesight, the Pleiades cluster is normally visible to the naked eye.

The constellation of Taurus is located in the Northern Hemisphere. It passes through the sky from November to March, but is most visible during the month of January. It covers 797 square degrees in the sky.

During the month of November, the Taurid meteor shower appears to radiate from the general direction of this constellation.

New insights into the meaning of Taurus?

O ur scientific knowledge of Taurus is lacking due to the distance of even the nearest planets in the constellation.

We do have additional data about many constellations from newly-invented high-powered telescopes. And modern space probes have added a great deal more to our collective knowledge base about many constellations just in the past few years.

But our understanding of what is in Taurus from a scientific vantage point is still quite vague.

An astrologer may well view this as a **planetary blind spot** or a **collective lack** in the area of Taurus in Earth's consciousness.

Or, in a more positive vein, an astrologer may view new information about other constellations as indicators of rapid human/Earth growth in the areas of consciousness and experience indicated by the nature of the constellations.

In the same vein, it is interesting that the brightest star in Taurus is **red**. Ever hear of the old saying about what happens when a bull sees red? A matador waves a red cape to entice the bull to fight. Many Earth languages today talk about an angry person who "sees red." Doubtlessly, these concepts trace origins in some way back to the bright red planet in Taurus the Bull.

Modern astrologers equate the color red more to Aries than Taurus. But the sky says otherwise.

It is worth noting that many ancient myths include male gods who appeared in the form of a bull to entice a beautiful maiden to ride on his back to trick her and lure her away. That the seven sisters appear on the shoulders of the bull, seems clearly related to those mythologies.

But there seems to be an internal riddle.

Modern Western astrology views Taurus as a feminine sign rather than a masculine sign.

And yet, in a similar way to the mythology of Aries, the cow in Taurus is male. It is explicitly referred to as a Bull, not just a cow.

The twist in Taurus, and perhaps why it is considered a feminine rather than masculine sign, is that **the STARS in the constellation are female**, not male.

It may be that the legends of why the seven sisters ride the bull have been corrupted or simply lost over time. Or removed for social or political reasons like Antinous may have been.

And then, it may simply point us towards the planetary blind spot.

Remember that in Taurus the shining stars are the seven women. But the constellation is named after the dishonest seducer, the Bull.

THE

CONSTELLATION OF

GEMINI

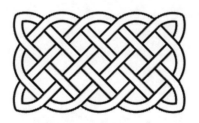

How Gemini was seen

in antiquity.

In Babylonian astronomy, the two main stars of Gemini were known as the **Great Twins**.

These twins were named **Meshlamtaea** and **Lugalirra**. The first name meant "the One Who Has Arisen from the Underworld." The second name meant "the Mighty King." Both names were considered titles of **Nergal**, the Babylonian God of **Plague** and **Pestilence**, who also was considered to be King of the Underworld.

Although we have no direct records of how the Babylonians perceived the nature of the twins, the mythology does seem a bit ominous.

In ancient Egypt, the sign of Gemini was called the "Two Stars" or Pimahi (meaning "the **United**").

To the Hebrews, the two stars were less important than the constellation itself, which they called Thaumin (also translated as "the united"). The glyph the Hebrews used for Gemini was a depiction of two wands bound together. It symbolized **conflicting positions bound together by compromise** and **duality mediated through intellect**.

In Greece, the two main stars of Gemini were named **Castor** and **Pollux**, the sons of the god Zeus and the beautiful mortal named Leda. Thus they were by nature a **mixture of the base and the divine**.

According to Greek legend, Leda was a devastatingly beautiful woman. A mortal woman. Zeus was the supreme god of the Greek Pantheon. And at the time he found Leda, he was married to his third wife—his third *immortal* wife—Hera. But that never stopped Zeus.

The legend says Leda was so incredibly beautiful that Zeus spotted her from his throne on Mount Olympus.

As many legends do, it has several variations. But the legend of the coupling of Zeus and Leda, and the subsequent birth of the twins Castor and Pollux, is one of the most chronicled unions in ancient Greece. It was mentioned by Homer in the *Iliad and the Odyssey*, Apollodorus in *Bibliotheca*,

Pausanias in *Description of Greece*, Hyginus in *Fabulae and Astronomica*, Virgil in *Aeneid*, and Ovid in *Metamorphoses*.

And it was a theme repeated by painters of many periods, down through the Renaissance.

But although there were four children born of the union, only two of them were twins: the inseparable Castor and Pollux with **a bond that could not be broken**. Well, almost not broken.

The two were together always, in one great adventure or war after another, both becoming great Greek heroes.

From the time they were very young, the twins were great warriors and valiant leaders. Together they victoriously led the Spartan army against Athens. They joined Jason and the Argonauts on the quest for the Golden Fleece. And side-by-side they were among the **brave hunters** of the great Calydonian Boar.

But as inseparable as they were, Castor and Pollux were **not created equal**.

Castor was a **great horseman**. Pollux had **extraordinary strength**.

But the most important difference was much greater than talents.

Castor was born mortal.

Pollux was born immortal.

When Castor was slain in battle, Pollux was inconsolable in his grief. He begged Zeus to relieve him of the bonds of immortality and allow him to die alongside his brother.

Zeus refused.

And yet, in his wisdom, Zeus solved Pollux's pain by granting Castor immortality as well.

Reunited in the heavens by the hand of Zeus himself, Castor and Pollux eternally stand in Gemini as a tribute to the depth and **selfless loyalty of brotherly love**.

Or thus most versions of the legend go.

For centuries sailors believed if the first night at sea they could see both Castor and Pollux, the journey would be prosperous. If they could see but one, it was a bad omen that the journey was ill-fated.

The 17th Century description of Gemini by British astrologer William Ramesey was:

> *The third sign is named Gemini (signifying Twins) because the Sun therein causeth a reduplication of heat; and all Creatures couple and in gender, every thing delighting in its mate.*

Clearly, by the 17th Century, the concept of Gemini had changed significantly.

84

What we know about the Constellation of Gemini today.

The constellation of Gemini looks remarkably like the mythological characters of the twins, **Castor** and **Pollux**, from Greek mythology. In fact, Gemini is one of the few constellations that actually looks like its namesake.

The two brightest stars in the constellation are thus named Castor and Pollux. These two stars are seen as the heads of the twins while fainter stars outline the two bodies. Pollux is an orange giant star 35 light-years from the earth; it is the brighter of the two twins' heads. Castor is actually a sextuplet star system 50 light-years from Earth that appears to us without massive magnification as a single star.

Gemini is one of the 48 constellations identified in the 2nd century by astronomer Ptolemy. It remains a constellation in today's modern list of constellations and is carved out in essentially the same part of the sky.

Gemini is relatively easy to spot in the night sky with the naked eye. It is located just northeast of Orion, between the constellations of Taurus and Cancer on the elliptic. It can be seen between the latitudes of 90 and -60 degrees. The best viewing in North America is during the month of February.

By April and May, Gemini can be seen soon after the sun sets in the western sky.

Since most people can locate the Big Dipper, even an amateur sky watcher can find Gemini by using the Big Dipper as a guide. Although the Big Dipper is actually an asterism, and not a true constellation, it is a very clear dipper-shaped pattern of stars always generally located in the north high on the sky's dome. If you draw an imaginary diagonal line through the bowl of the Big Dipper, from the star **Megrez** through the star **Merak**, heading the direction opposite of the Big Dipper's handle, the line will point directly to the two brightest stars of Gemini, Castor and Pollux.

Although Castor and Pollux are traditionally referred to in that order, it is actually Pollux that is the brighter star. In fact Pollux is the brightest star in the constellation, with Castor the second brightest.

Pollux is an orange-giant star approximately 35 light-years from Earth. It has a magnitude of 1.14 and also has an extra-solar planet revolving around it.

While appearing to the eye as a 1.6 magnitude blue-white star, Castor is actually not a star, but a sextuplet star system. It is located between 50 light-years and 52 light-years from Earth, depending on which of the sixteen stars we measure the distance to. Castor has two spectroscopic binary stars visible at magnitudes of 1.9 and 3.0 with a period of 470 years. It also has a wide-set red dwarf star that is an Algo-type eclipsing binary star with a magnitude ranging from 9.8 at a minimum to 9.3 at a maximum with a period of 19.5 years.

Much of Gemini is easily visible.

The constellation of Gemini contains an astounding 85 stars visible to the naked eye without a telescope.

Double stars, binary stars, and exoplanets in Gemini.

In addition to Pollux having an orbiting planet, at least two other stars in Gemini have orbiting planets as well, HD 50554 and HD 59686.

The constellation of Gemini is also the home of **Alhena**, a blue-white star 105 light-years from Earth with a magnitude of 1.9.

Also in Gemini is **Wasat**, a long-period binary star. Wasat's primary star is white with a magnitude of 3.5. Its secondary star is an orange dwarf at magnitude 8.2. Wasat is 59 light-years from Earth and its period is more than 1,000 years. It is not visible to the naked eye, but most moderate-grade amateur telescopes can pick it up.

Gemini also includes the double star **Mebsuta**. Its primary star is a yellow super-giant located 900 light-years from Earth that shines with a magnitude of 3.1. The companion star is brighter in our sky with a magnitude of 9.6 and is visible with a small telescope or even a pair of binoculars.

Propus is a variable binary star 380 light-years away. Visible only with the aid of larger amateur telescopes, it has a period of 500 years. The primary star is a semi-regular red

WHERE ALPHA MEETS OMEGA

giant with a period of 233 days and a magnitude ranging from 3.9 at minimum to 3.1 at maximum. Its visual companion star has a magnitude of 6.0.

Two other significant binary stars are found in Gemini. One is **kGem** at 143 light-years from Earth. Its primary is a yellow giant visible at 3.6 magnitude, with a secondary star of 8.0. Both are seen only using commercial or high-quality amateur telescopes due to discrepancy in visual brightness. And the other is referred to as **38 Gem**, 84 light-years from Earth and visible with binoculars. The primary star of 38 Gem is a 4.8 magnitude white star with a yellow secondary star of 7.8 magnitude.

And still another significant double star in Gemini is **vGem**. Its primary star is a blue giant with a magnitude of 4.1 that is 550 light-years from Earth. The secondary star in vGem has a magnitude of 8.0.

Gemini is filled with meteor showers.

There are 11 meteor showers that radiate from Gemini in any given year.

The most spectacular of these meteor showers is probably the **Geminids**. They occur at the end of the year, peaking about the 13th or 14th of December. What makes the Geminids especially interesting is that

they are multi-colored rather than all just one
color

Other notable findings in Gemini.

Several other noteworthy astronomical
anomalies exist in Gemini.

Gemini includes a star called Mekbuda that is a super-
giant star with a radius close to 220,000 times the size of
the Sun.

Mekbuda is actually still another double
star, the main star of which is a yellow super-
giant 1,200 light-years from Earth that is a
Cepheid variable star with a period of 10.2
days and a magnitude ranging from 4.2 to
3.6. It is the star that is 220,000 times the
size of our Sun. Mekbuda's optical
companion has a magnitude of 7.6 and is
visible with an amateur telescope or even
with binoculars.

There also is an object in Gemini called
Geminga that astronomers tell us is a
neutron star. Neutron stars like Geminga are
stars with a very small radius, typically no
more than eighteen miles, and a very high
density. They are thought to be composed of
closely packed neutrons formed by the
gravitational collapse of a massive star after
supernova explosion. If enough debris is left
after this kind of supernova explosion, a

black hole would be left in the place rather than a neutron star.

Nearby Geminga are the Eskimo Nebula and Medusa Nebula. The Eskimo Nebula, also known as the Clown Nebula, has gas clouds that are so complex our scientists really aren't sure what they are.

Additionally, there is a Messier object named M35 that was found by French astronomer Charles Messier in 1771. M35 is a star cluster located near the feet of the twins that astronomers today estimate is more than 100 million years old.

And, along with an unusually high number of **binary and double stars**, Gemini contains a dwarf nova-type cataclysmic variable star referred to as **U Gem** that was discovered in 1855 by astronomer J.R. Hind.

Gemini's connection with discovery.

Interestingly, in his great work *Meteorologica*, Aristotle mentions that he observed Jupiter in conjunction with an occulting star in the constellation of Gemini. That reference was the earliest known observation of the its kind. Modern astronomers tell us the date of the observation was likely December 5, 337 B.C.

And it also was in Gemini that Uranus was "discovered" by astronomer William Herschel on March 13, 1781.

New insights into the meaning of Gemini?

O ne of the first things we might note about Gemini is that despite the common order of the pair of names, Castor and Pollux, it is Pollux that is the brightest star in the constellation. Not Castor.

It was Pollux who was born immortal, blessed with legendary strength, infused with the Divine. And in the sky, it is Pollux that is the brightest star.

Castor was not graced with Pollux's strength. Castor was a great horseman, more in touch with animal nature than the Divine. He was base, of the mortal world. And in the sky, Castor shines more dimly than Pollux.

Perhaps that is just a cosmic coincidence.

Perhaps.

But somehow, without our modern telescopes the ancients saw the "double" energy in the sky where Gemini sits. And now we know it is a constellation filled with double stars and binary stars.

Another coincidence perhaps.

The ominous "arising from the underworld" as seen by the Babylonians and the relationship with plague and pestilence seem very out of place with the modern concept of Gemini.

And while the ancient Hebrew concept of Gemini **binding together conflicting views through compromise** and of **intellect mediating duality** feels familiar to our modern concept, the richness of its wisdom is seldom a major theme in modern astrological interpretation of Gemini.

But it does give significant food for thought—particularly since this thread of compromise and intellect rising above is part of the ancient mythology of two great warriors.

THE

CONSTELLATION OF

CANCER

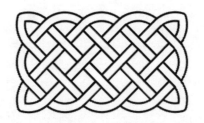

How Cancer was seen

in antiquity.

In Egyptian records from about 2000 B.C., Cancer was described as a **scarab**. To the Egyptians, the scarab was the **sacred emblem of immortality**.

Cancer is said to have been the place for the Akkadian "Sun of the South." Now remember, this was a long, long way back in time since Akkadia pre-dated Babylonia, which in turn pre-dated Greece, which in turn pre-dated ancient Rome. But in centuries following the Akkadian civilization, and possibly after a major axis shift of the Earth, Cancer was then known as the northern gate of the sun rather than of the southern sun.

In Babylonia, the constellation of Cancer was known as Mul.Al.Lul, a name which can refer both to a **crab** and to a **snapping turtle**. On boundary stones in Babylonia, the image of a **turtle** or **tortoise** appears quite regularly and it is believed that this represents Cancer since the conventional crab has not so far been discovered on any of these monuments. There also appears to be a strong connection between the Babylonian constellation and ideas of death in a passage to the underworld, which may be the origin of these ideas in later Greek myths associated with Heracles and the Hydra.

Since so few stars are visible in Cancer, it was often considered the "**dark sign**." It was quaintly described as black and without eyes.

By the time we get to Greek mythology, the constellation of Cancer is identified by the giant crab that Heracles (whom the Romans later called Hercules) accidentally stepped on while fighting the many-headed Hydra. In self-defense, the frightened crab grabbed onto Heracles' toe and Heracles responded by crushing the crab under his foot. After the battle was over, the legend continues with the goddess **Hera**, a sworn enemy of Heracles, who felt so badly about what Heracles had done to the crab that she put the poor creature's body in the sky for eternity as the constellation of Cancer.

At least that's one version. As in all legends, there are several variations.

Another variation of the Greek legend is that the crab **Karkinos** was sent by enemies of Heracles, Hera herself in some stories, to distract Heracles and put him at a disadvantage during the battle with the Hydra. But Heracles quickly reacted by kicking the crab with such great force that it was propelled into the sky.

We know that the ancient Greek Erastus, who is mentioned in the Bible and who is considered by the Greek Orthodox Church to be one of the Seventy Disciples of Jesus, called Cancer a crab. So did Hipparchus and Ptolemy.

The amazing Greek Eratosthenes curiously called Cancer the "**Crab, Asses, and Crib.**" If you have no clue what Eratosthenes' phrase means, you are in good company because most historians aren't sure either.

In ancient Rome, various classical writers signified Cancer as a **crab**, **lobster**, or even **scorpion**.

One of the few constants of the constellation of Cancer over the centuries has been a **creature with an exoskeleton**, or at least with a partial exoskeleton. There also has, for the most part, been a repeated theme of a creature **living in water** or one able to live in water part of the time.

Some scholars have suggested that the crab was a late addition to the myth of Heracles in order to make the twelve labors correspond with the twelve signs of the zodiac. This may be why there seems to be an inconsistent legend in the ancient Greek world. And it also may be an explanation for the multitude of crustaceans associated with the constellation over the eons.

The root of the constellation of Cancer, like the sea itself, is deep and murky.

But there does seem to be a repetition of a crab-like creature from some of our very earliest records. And this more ancient mythological creature may be the real reason for the non-uniform attempt at describing it in recognizable terms.

In the very earliest concepts, many antiquarians say Cancer was associated with **Bythos** (meaning "sea depths") and **Aphros** (meaning "sea foam") who were collectively called the *Ichothynes*. These two gods were **Ichthyocentaurs**, or what we might call Fish-Centaurs. They had the upper bodies of men, the lower fore-quarters of horses, the serpentine tails of fish, and foreheads with lobster claws growing out of them. They are widely depicted in art ranging from mosaics found in the ancient city of Zeugma to the famous classical painting of *The Birth of*

Venus by Italian painter Sandro Botticelli (c. 1842) that now is housed in the Uffizi Museum in Florence, Italy.

Bythos and Aphros are considered by most mythologers as the same two fish placed in the heavens to form the constellation of Pisces. But their association with Venus (Aphrodite) seems to wind repeatedly throughout mythology.

In the 12th century an illustrated astronomical manuscript depicts Cancer as a **water beetle**.

And in a 1488 Latin translation, Cancer appears as a **large crayfish**. "Crayfish," by the way, is the constellation's name in most Germanic languages.

In the 17th century, German and Polish astronomers described Cancer as a **lobster**. But in the same century, the English astrologer William Ramesey's much more clinical description clearly saw Cancer as a **crab**. In Ramesey's seminal work *Astrologia Restaurata* (published in London in 1653) he wrote of Cancer:

> *The fourth sign is called Cancer (signifying a Crab) because the Sun being therein, goeth, as it were, backward, (after the nature of the Crab) retiring*

towards the Equinoctial from whence he came, declining contrary to that of the Twins.

The variances of Cancer symbolism have been pretty much literally "all over the map" for centuries, even well into modern times.

But of course, we all know Western astrologers today widely share the concept that Cancer is represented by the Crab, and particularly the pinchers of the crab.

What we know about the Constellation of Cancer today.

The constellation of Cancer is the dimmest of constellations of the zodiac. It has only two stars brighter than the fourth magnitude. Yet despite its dimness, it is the 31st of the 88 constellations in the Earth's sky and was one of the constellations cataloged by the Greek astronomer Ptolemy in the 2nd century.

Cancer lies between Leo and Gemini. With the naked eye or even with binoculars, it is almost impossible to actually see a crab when you look at the constellation of Cancer in the sky. It usually appears more as an upside down Y.

Cancer is visible in the northern hemisphere in the early spring, and in the southern hemisphere during autumn. The constellation of Cancer occupies an area of 506 square degrees in the sky. The best visibility in the northern hemisphere is during March about 9 PM.

The brightest star in Cancer is the rare Al Tarf.

The brightest star in Cancer is an orange K-type giant star named **Al Tarf** with the magnitude of 3.5. It is located 290 light-years from Earth and is difficult to see in the sky without a telescope.

Al Tarf is 61 times the size of our home star, the Sun, and 660 times as bright. It was known to the ancient Arabic astrologers and still bears the name given to it in Arabia. Today we know Al Tarf is actually a binary star with a much fainter 14th magnitude companion called Beta Cancri. They orbit each other once every 76,000 years.

The name Al Tarf comes from the Arabic word for "edge" or the "end." And it is indeed located on the edge of Cancer, in the left bottom foot of the crab towards the end of the constellation.

Scientists tell us Al Tarf is approximately 2 billion years old. And today we know it has an orbiting planet with a 605-day orbit. That orbiting planet's size, based on its orbital velocity, is 7.8 times the mass of Jupiter.

Another interesting note is that Cancer's brightest star Al Tarf is a barium star, a specific class of cool giant stars whose atmospheres contain high levels of barium. Barium stars are thought to be the products of convection currents caused by a donor star that blew off its upper layers in its evolution. Barium stars typically also contain high levels of zirconium and zirconium oxide. They have been a conundrum for our scientists for many years.

Other exoplanets in the constellation of Cancer.

The constellation of Cancer has numerous exoplanets.

The most well-known is 55 Cancri e, a super earth that was identified as a "diamond world" when it was found in 2004. However, follow-up studies in 2013 suggest there is far less carbon in the planet than originally thought, so the concept of a diamond planet may not have been correct. The exact nature of the planet's surface is still unclear.

We do know, however, that 55 Cancri, the yellow double star that 55 Cancri e orbits, actually has at least five extra-solar planets in orbit around it. So 55 Cancri e is not a lone planet circling a sun.

But what makes the five planets orbiting 55 Cancri really interesting is that they are splayed into several solar systems, including ours, as well as into other signs of the Zodiac in our sky beyond the constellation of Cancer.

The nearest to Earth of these five planets is a planet believed to be a terrestrial planet with a mass close to that of Neptune.

The outermost planets circling 55 Cancri are believed to be Jovian planets with masses similar to that of Jupiter.

Cancer is filled with extremely distant sky objects and star clusters.

The constellation of Cancer contains a large number of famous deep sky objects.

One is an open star cluster called *Praesepe* made up of more than 200 stars (although only about 50 are visible without a large telescope) that also is known as the **"Beehive Cluster."** It is categorized as a Messier object and often is scientifically referred to as M44. All three names refer to the same star cluster. To the eye, this cluster resembles **a swarm of bees**. The brightest in the cluster is the sixth magnitude. Overall, the cluster has an apparent magnitude of 3.7. It sits 577 light-years from Earth. It is one of the nearest open clusters to Earth and typically can be seen without binoculars on a very clear night. Its arc is 95 minutes across.

The best time to view it in the Northern Hemisphere is when Cancer is high in the sky, between February and May.

Another Messier object visible in Cancer is an open star cluster referred to as M67, or the **"King Cobra Cluster"** located in the northernmost part of the sign. It appears approximately the same size as a full moon. The King Cobra has an apparent magnitude of 6.1 and it falls between 2,600 and a little more than 2,900 light-years from Earth. You can find it roughly halfway between *Regulus* (in Leo) and *Procyon* (in Canis Minor, a non-zodiac constellation). Scientists tell us it is one of the oldest open clusters known with an **estimated age of between 3.2 billion and 5 billion years old**.

The King Cobra Cluster contains more than 100 stars similar to our Sun as well as a number of red giant stars.

Since most of the stars in the King Cobra Cluster are about the same age and the same distance from Earth—with the exception of about 30 or so blue "stragglers"—it is one of the most studied sky objects by scientists studying stellar evolution.

Other interesting findings about Cancer.

Another truly fascinating object in Cancer, based on observations by NASA and the Hubble Space Telescope, is an object called NGC 2775, or Caldwell 48. This is a rare spiral b galaxy about 55.5 million light-years from Earth with an apparent magnitude of 11.03. First discovered by William Herschel in 1783, scientists now suspect there has been recent star-forming activity occurring within it.

Two supernovae were recently observed in the constellation of Cancer. SN 1920A peaked at a magnitude of 11.7 in December of 1920. And SN 2001bg was observed in May of 2001, to peak shortly thereafter at a magnitude of 13.7.

New insights into the meaning of Cancer?

In sifting through the mythology surrounding the sign of Cancer, the clearly repeating theme is lack of clarity.

And yes, that sentence is an oxymoron.

But then, in many ways, that may be the over-arching historical theme of Cancer.

Even the astronomical data we have gathered about the constellation seem imbued with that concept.

At least five known planets circle a star in Cancer that appear in our sky in several different constellations—and that we know actually cross into several other solar systems as well as ours!

That combined with the fact that the brightest star in Cancer is a rare and curious barium star, a kind of star that is a scientific conundrum to our scientists...

And even where the constellation of Cancer itself **appears in the sky** seems to have been a question mark. Remember, the early Akkadians first recorded the Sun in Cancer as being in the South. And then later in Akkadian history, the Sun in Cancer was said to be in the North.

Clarity and certainty are not repeating themes here.

No wonder the constellation was seen in so many different ways over the eons.

One wonders if the modern vestige of the Crab who moves in a non-direct zigzag pattern might not stem from this same kind of energy. And then, of course, there is the modern Cancerian association with the constantly inconstant Moon and the tie to an ever-changing emotional nature of man...

But more than an oxymoron or conundrum or paradox, there seems to be an aspect of Cancer that has been lost in the mist of Time. Something simply feels "missing."

A mystic friend of mine says some of the most profound discoveries of the next two centuries will come from the constellation of Cancer. We, of course, have no way of knowing how true this may be, but the sheer age and size of what we have found in Cancer is difficult to wrap our brains around.

That there are **more than 100 stars** in one star cluster of Cancer alone that are **larger than our Sun**— is something we humans have a difficult time imagining. And it certainly challenges our concepts of the universe only a few decades ago.

The dark sign without eyes—seems to remain difficult for us to see or fully comprehend.

THE

CONSTELLATION OF

LEO

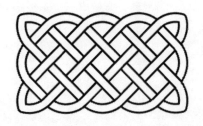

How Leo was seen in antiquity.

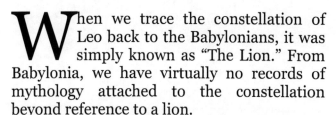

When we trace the constellation of Leo back to the Babylonians, it was simply known as "The Lion." From Babylonia, we have virtually no records of mythology attached to the constellation beyond reference to a lion.

In fact, unlike many constellations that have morphed in symbolism considerably over time, the Babylonians, the Persians, the Turks, the Syrians, the Hebrews, and the Indians all used words for this constellation that meant the lion.

But by the time of the Greeks, the mythology surrounding Leo begins to get complicated. The lion remains prominent, but the stories around it and about it become complex.

WHERE ALPHA MEETS OMEGA

Two competing Greek myths of Leo.

We have two ancient competing myths about the constellation of Leo.

One appears to be from the Greeks. And the other appears to be from the Romans. But of that, we are not certain.

Of course, we know that the Romans are famous for taking Greek legends and simply re-telling them with Roman names. But Leo seems to be an exception. By Roman times, there clearly was a competing myth around the constellation of Leo that evolved side-by-side with the a Greek myth clothed in Roman names.

Historians seems to be split on whether these dual myths originated in Greece or if the competing myth was created solely by the Romans. The "second" myth seems to only have been recorded in words by a Roman. But, of course, that in no way gives certainty that it was not a myth from Greece we simply have no record of today.

But the two myths do seem very different in how they characterize the lion and the circumstances surrounding the lion.

The myth of Heracles/Hercules and the Nemean Lion.

113

One of the myths says the name of the constellation of Leo comes from the **Nemean Lion** that the great hero Heracles slew in an epic battle. The story of the Nemean Lion is one in a series of Greek tales that later became known as the **Twelve Labors of Heracles**.

Of course, you may have heard of this as the Twelve Labors of *Hercules*. The myths about Hercules actually were a Roman re-telling of tales about the earlier Greek hero of Heracles whose name has been eclipsed over the eons by the name Hercules. But the roots of the Nemean Lion legend are Greek and a tale of one of the triumphs of Heracles. And despite the close association with Heracles and the constellation of Leo, the Nemean Lion battle was only one of the "labors" and superhuman trials Heracles went through.

But to fully understand the myth of Heracles, and the basis of the constellation of Leo, we need to understand Heracles' birth and what led up to the Twelve Labors.

Heracles's father was the immortal King of the Gods Zeus himself. Zeus had a long history of cheating on his wife Hera. And Hera was well known for her jealousy, with good reason.

In one of Zeus's most dastardly seductions, he turned himself into the likeness of the husband of a beautiful mortal princess named Alcmene and tricked her into bed by his appearance. She thought she had fallen into bed with her husband. But, of course, the truth came out. And it soon became obvious to all of the gods on Olympus that Alcmene was pregnant with Zeus's son. Hera was livid. Then, possibly as part of his ongoing war with his wife Hera, Zeus decreed the next of his sons to be born would succeed him as king. Hera flew into a rage and through a magical trick delayed Heracles's birth to insure **Eurystheus** was born before Heracles. Then, to double down, Hera sent two magical serpents to kill the baby Heracles as he lay sleeping in his cradle. The first trial, and the first superhuman victory, of Heracles was his strangling of the two magical snakes as a baby.

And as it turns out, even though Heracles was not Hera's son, as he grew older it became obvious Heracles shared Hera's awful temper.

According to legend, Heracles was a great warrior and as reward after a great victory married the daughter of a mortal king. But Hera, not satisfied to see Heracles successful or happy, cursed him with temporary insanity causing him to kill his wife and children in the rage. For that indiscretion, Heracles was sentenced to be the personal slave of (now) ***King*** **Eurystheus**. Urged on by Hera's anger, Eurystheus ordered a series of trials, later collectively called the Twelve

Labors, fully believing that Heracles could never live through them.

But of course, he did.

The Nemean Lion was the first of these trials. At least the first of the trials of the adult Heracles.

In the Nemean Lion and Heracles story, the **fearsome** lion was **terrorizing** the world and killing all who encountered it. This lion was far larger, stronger, and more fierce than any lion mankind had previously encountered. The lion's claws were stronger and sharper than any sword, and his skin was impervious to arrows or metal of any sort, so he was impossible for men to kill. Even the arrows of the god Heracles bounced off of the great Nemean lion. So Heracles abandoned his weapons and **relied upon himself** and **his own strength**. He wrestled the lion with his bare hands and strangled the Nemean Lion to death.

Then, upon realizing the magical power in the lion's skin and wanting to bring the skin back to King Eurystheus as proof of the kill, Heracles attempted to skin the lion. His sword could not piece the lion's skin. No outer tools worked. So Heracles removed one of the lion's claws and skinned the lion with the lion's own claw—forever after to wear the Nemean Lion's skin as an impervious cloak.

Interestingly enough, the constellation of Leo appears to be an homage to the *lion*, not the hero—unlike most constellation legends.

Some antiquarians point to a line of Greek legends that say Hera had the magical lion created in the first place and sent it to Nemea to keep worshipers away from a great temple to Zeus after a previous "indiscretion" of Zeus'. And the conjecture of these historians is that it was Hera's hand that robbed Heracles from the constellation and put the lion in the place of honor instead.

Self-reliance summons superhuman strength. And yet, **Jealousy** and **rage**, even if justified, are powerful forces that can negate even the most wonderful acts.

The myth of Pyramus, Thisbe, the mulberry tree, and the lion.

The other line of myths comes from the Roman poet Ovid's tale of **Pyramus** and **Thisbe** (written some time between 1 B.C. and 1 A.D.).

As the tale goes, the two young lovers Pyramus and Thisbe were separated by their parents who felt they were too young to marry. But in an effort to get around their parents, the two agreed to meet secretly by a **mulberry tree** filled with white berries.

When Thisbe arrived for their meeting, wearing a veil to hide her identity along her journey to the mulberry tree, a huge lion sprang from behind the tree. And as Thisbe hurriedly ran away, she dropped her veil as she ran. The lion, still bloody from his last kill, pounced upon the veil, tearing it to shreds and as he was doing so, Pyramus arrived. Shocked and heart-broken, Pyramus immediately assumed his love was dead and unable to bear the thought of living without her, threw himself on his sword to his death. But Thisbe heard his screams and returned to find Pyramus lying in a pool of his own **blood**. As he lay dying at her feet, she took his sword and killed herself next to him.

As the legend goes, the tragic blood that was spilled that day colored the berries of the mulberry red.

By this legend, Leo has a sinister and tragic element of causation that in itself does not kill, but rather causes such **fear and despair** that violent and horrible consequences flow from it. Tragedy stems from **mistake**, not from the lion himself.

Any takers that William Shakespeare had studied Greek mythology?

By the 17th Century, the Zodiac sign of Leo seems to have taken on a different concept.

As summarized in 1653 by the British astrologer William Ramesey in *Astrologia Restaurata*:

The fifth sign is called Leo (signifying a Lion) because the Sun being therein, the heat is there increased in great strength and dryness, after the nature of the Lion, which is of a strong, hot and dry nature.

What we know about the Constellation of Leo today.

Leo is one of the earliest recognized constellations. And it is the 12th largest of our modern 88 constellations. One of the reasons it is so easily seen is the presence of a number of really bright stars.

The constellation of Leo lies between Cancer to the west and Virgo to the east. It is visible in the Northern Hemisphere about the time of the spring equinox and remains easily identifiable through most of the months of April and May, with its clearest visibility during the month of April around 9 PM.

Leo is a highly recognizable constellation, one of the few that actually resembles its namesake. It's easy to find in the sky because of the pointer stars in the Big Dipper—which point to Leo. Although some say that stars comprising the chest and the neck of the lion appear to more resemble a sickle than a lion.

One of the brightest stars in Leo is in the curve of the sickle, **Al Geiba**. Al Geiba and two other stars form a triangle of stars that create the lion's haunches. The brightest star in this trio is named **Denebola**, meaning "tail of the lion" in Arabic.

The constellation of Leo is visually prominent in the sky.

Leo has four star of the first or second magnitude. So it is bright.

The brightest star in Leo is **Regulus**, or " the Little King." Regulus is a main-sequence blue-white star with a magnitude of 1.34. It is 77.5 light-years from Earth and actually is a double star. Its secondary star has a magnitude of 7.7.

The second brightest star in Leo is **Denebola**, or "the Lion's Tail." And as you might expect from its name, it is located at the opposite end of the constellation from

Regulus. Denebola is a blue-white star of magnitude 2.23, 36 light-years from Earth.

Located in the forehead or the mane of the lion, depending on the scholar's description, is the star **Al Gieba**. Sometimes referred to as *Algieba*, this is a binary star with a third optical component. Two of the stars can be seen with a small telescope. The third can be seen with ordinary binoculars. The main star of Al Gieba is a gold-yellow giant with a magnitude 2.61.The secondary star is similar to the primary, but with a magnitude of 3.6. The third is a yellow-tinged star of magnitude 4.8.

Zosma, named for the Greek word meaning "the Girdle," is located on the back of the lion. It also is called by the Arabic name Dhur of the same meaning. Zosma is actually a very rare pale yellow, blue, and violet triple star with an apparent magnitude of 2.58 that is located 58 light-years from Earth.

Leo has a large number of exoplanets in it.

Recent discoveries show a plethora of exoplanets in Leo, including at least one that is potentially habitable.

But the more discoveries that are made in the Leo constellation, the more scientists learn of the strange anomalies in it. And the more questions are raised.

Strange anomalies in the constellation of Leo.

Starting in 2008, astronomers noted a planet orbiting a dying red giant star about 1,200 light-years away from Earth that they noted was extremely bloated. Astronomers noted it would be "an interesting topic for a follow-up."

Then in 2010, astronomers discovered a large planet called GJ 436b.

And in 2015, they announced that the planet GJ 436b appears to be roughly 22 times the size of Earth and has a huge gas cloud streaming away from it for millions of miles.

Continued observations over the next two years revealed that the planet has a bizarre orbit that actually goes over the star's poles. This kind of planetary behavior is strikingly different from anything we find in our own solar system. In our solar system planets' orbits gather around the Sun's equator, not is poles.

Then in late 2017, astronomers found a potentially rocky exoplanet in Leo they named K2-18b that appears to be orbiting in the habitable zone of its red dwarf star. This means that liquid water could exist on the surface of K2-18b. It appears the planet is about 2.2 times bigger than Earth. And astronomers are not certain if what they are seeing is the ice shell of a water world or simply a rocky world with a thin atmosphere.

The constellation of Leo contains a number of luminous galaxies within it.

Meteor showers in Leo.

Between January 1 and January 7 of every year, the "January Leones" peak in the Northern Hemisphere. They are a relatively minor but predictable meteor shower in the constellation of Leo.

The big meteor shower in Leo occurs in November and peaks November 14-15 in the Northern Hemisphere. The "Leonids" have a huge outburst every 35 years at a normal peak rate of about 10 meteors every hour.

As with all meteor showers, the best time to watch is between midnight and dawn when the sky is at its darkest.

New insights into the meaning of Leo?

That the stars in Leo shine exceptionally brightly or that the constellation of Leo contains many luminous galaxies. Those scientific findings certainly fit with our modern concept of Leo and are not surprising to a student of astrology.

It is the ancient information that raises questions.

Several themes or "lessons" seem to leap out when we read about the ancient mythology of Leo.

One of the first things we see about Leo through the eyes of the ancients is the **outer source of fear** and the facing of a **terrifying enemy of greater size and**

strength not just with courage, but with **internal strength**.

In these old myths, the concept that **strength comes from within** and that **self-reliance** can triumph against all odds seems to reverberate. Not relying on an arrow or a spear or a knife, but taking it on with our bare hands—that is where victory lies, no matter how fierce the opponent. Or so seem to say the myths.

Although one could make a case these ideas are still part of modern Leo in a *way*, the truth is we seldom look at Leo in that light today. It certainly isn't the primary meaning most astrologers ascribe to Leo.

Another aspect of the old mythology that seems to touch only the periphery of the modern concept of Leo is the horror of **jealousy** and **rage** and **the awful damage they can do** both to oneself and to others. Both anger and jealousy certainly are creatures of the ego. But we have greatly lost those as concepts of Leo. Or dangers of Leo.

And then, the other theme that seems to beg for attention is that **fear** and **despair** can lead to **horrible mistake** with long-ranging and dire consequences.

In modern astrology, we look at Leo as brave. But we often forget that bravery does not mean the absence of fear. It simply means using fear in the right way—like running away from a hungry lion—and not letting fear become panic and despair, and destruction.

Had Pyramus simply taken a beat, had he not acted rashly out of panic and despair, he would have found Thisbe safe and sound. And they may well have lived to babysit their grandchildren. Instead they both died in a pool of blood. The mulberry tree may have benefited, but certainly no one else did.

There seem to be deep moral lessons embedded in these old Leo myths that lie only on the edges of our modern concept of Leo.

Perhaps these ancient meanings have gradually been lost because mankind has mastered these lessons.

But   probably   not.

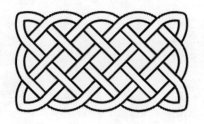

THE

CONSTELLATION OF

VIRGO

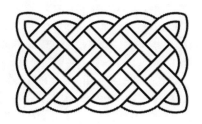

How Virgo was seen in

antiquity.

The Greek astronomer, geographer, and mathematician Hipparchus (190 B.C.-120 B.C.) tells us that the constellation of Virgo was two separate constellations in the Babylonian times.

But from archaeological records we have pieced together from other sources as well, that was true for *part* of Babylonian times. But what constituted "the zodiac" was fluid even for the Babylonian. Very far back in the Babylonian world, there were as many as eighteen signs in the Babylonian Zodiac. The number gradually decreased to twelve in the last known revision of the Babylonian MUL.APIN.

Uniting the "two Virgos" appears to have been one of the last revisions.

One of what we today would call "the Virgos" was called the AB.SIN, or the "**Furrow**," located in what is now the eastern sector of Virgo. And the other was the "**Frond of Low Erua**" in the Western sector of modern Virgo. In the final revision of the MUL.APIN, the Frond was united with the Furrow. But understanding the more ancient division can give us a great deal of insight into both ancient thought and the sign's deeper meaning.

We still have records from the Babylonian MUL.APIN (10th century BC), about the "the Furrow." Although the word *furrow* is seldom used in modern English, a furrow is a long, narrow trench made in the ground by a plow made especially either for planting seeds or for irrigation.

The constellation of the Furrow in ancient Babylonia was represented the goddess **Shala** and her **ear of grain**. To the Babylonians, the Furrow represented **fertility**. Depictions of the Furrow show a standing goddess holding an ear of grain.

The Babylonian constellation of the Frond of Low Erua was depicted by **a goddess holding a palm frond**—a motif that still occasionally appears in later descriptions of Virgo. To the Babylonians, the palm frond was sacred. It gave shade, dates, consolation, and calm. And if traversing a desert area, it meant water was close by.

One star in his constellation, **Spica**, retains the Babylonian meaning even today. The word spica is the Latin word for "ear of grain." Grain, and in particular a type of maize similar to our modern corn, was one of the major agricultural products of the Mesopotamian Delta in Babylon. Their diet and a large part of their economy was based on it.

Exactly when and how these two constellation merged into the modern constellation of Virgo is not certain. But we know by the time Ptolemy created his map of the heavenly constellations in the 2nd Century A.D., the constellation was simply listed as Virgo, not two separate constellations.

Multiple female deities have been associated with Virgo over the eons.

Early Greek astronomy associated the Babylonian constellation of Eura with their goddess of wheat and agriculture, **Demeter**.

The Romans associated it with their goddess **Ceres**. Ceres' name derives from the reconstructed Proto-Indo-European root word *kerh*, meaning "to satiate, to feed", which is also the root for Latin word crescere, which means "to grow." Roman etymologists believe the word *ceres* to be derived from the Latin verb gerere, which means "to **bear, bring forth, produce**."

Another goddess commonly associated with the constellation of Virgo is the Greek goddess **Persephone**, the daughter of Zeus and Demeter who was seduced to go to the Underworld by Hades when he appeared to her disguised as a beautiful white bull while she was innocently picking flowers in a spring field. Hades enticed Persephone to climb upon his back and stole her away.

Once in the Underworld with Hades, the legend says Persephone ate of the beautiful red **pomegranate**—thereby symbolizing the consummation of her "lawful" marriage to Hades since she had "partaken of his fruit."

Hades refused to send Persephone back above ground no matter how much she or her mother Demeter begged. His argument was that the "marriage" had been consummated with that pomegranate and therefore Persephone was "his."

In that myth, according to astrologer and antiquarian Eleanor Bach, Demeter (Ceres to the Romans) **"went on strike"** and denied the world Spring until her daughter was returned above the ground to Earth. All life on Earth was frozen in perpetual Winter and no new life could emerge. Seeds could not sprout and babies could not be born. Goddesses are powerful like that. And mothers get that angry when their children are mistreated.

So the Earth was thrown into perpetual Winter by a furious mother. To restore the balance of nature, Zeus had to step in and broker a truce between Demeter and Hades.

The result was that Persephone would forever stay with her "husband" for half of the year (Winter) and would come above ground to the Earth to be with her mother for the other half of the year (Summer). In that way the balance of the world was restored. And Persephone was viewed as the **Goddess of Spring**.

In Roman mythology, a nearly identical legend exists, but the names of the mother and daughter are Ceres and Prosperina instead of Demeter and Persephone.

But these were not the only goddesses associated with Virgo.

According to many Greek legends, **Astraea** (the daughter of *Themis*) went up to heaven to become the constellation of Virgo and carried the Scales of Justice with her.

Today we think of the Scales of Justice as part of Libra, because it is, but it wasn't during the time of the Greeks. It was in Virgo. And it was a major part of Virgo.

Not to get ahead of ourselves here, but Virgo and Scorpio both got "robbed" by the

Romans to create the "new" constellation of Libra. The portion of Astraea that was sectioned off for the new constellation by the Romans included the portion of the sky with the scales. Through this Roman re-sectioning, the scales became a part of Libra, not of Virgo. But at one time, the Scales of Justice were in Virgo.

Multiple legends going back as far as the first century B.C. speak of **maidens** and **virgins** who were relegated to the heavens. But one important note here, the "virgins" referred to in antiquity were viewed as fertile and ripe although usually innocent and young. There was no connotation of coldness or frigidity often associated with the sign today. In fact, the concept of a virgin in antiquity was the polar opposite of barren—it was the prime of fertility.

During the Middle Ages, Virgo became associated with the **Blessed Virgin Mary**. More likely than not, this was a societal extension of the previous symbolism of a pure young maiden simply given a Christian makeover. We find these kinds of Christian overlays repeated through the signs of the Zodiac.

Virgo as it was summarized by William Ramesey in 1653:

134

The fifth sign is called Virgo (signifying a maid) because the Sun therein hath his heat diminished, and dryness ruleth, so that things cease to increase, and the earth becometh barren; being of the nature of a Virgin, who is naturally tending to cold rather than heat, and is of herself barren.

This description, as you can see, varies significantly with the more ancient descriptions of Virgo. It seems to pare out a small part of the Demeter and Persephone myth and ignore other parts. And yet, as incomplete as it is, this concept is now deeply embedded in Western astrology.

What we know about

the Constellation of

Virgo today.

The constellation of Virgo is the second largest constellation in the sky and **the largest of the astrological constellations**. And before part of Virgo was carved out to create the constellation of Libra, it was the largest of the constellations.

Today, Virgo covers 1,294 square degrees of sky.

It's a congested constellation with at least a dozen Messier objects and dozens of exoplanets.

Although most of the stars in the constellation of Virgo are dim, the bright blue star **Spica** is easy to locate in the sky with the naked eye. If you follow the curve of the handle and the Big Dipper down to the southeast you come to the bright star *Arcturus* in the Boötes constellation. And then from *Arcturus* you simply continue the arc to the next bright star, and that is *Spica*.

Virgo appears in the Northern Hemisphere during the spring and summer, and in the Southern Hemisphere in autumn and winter. The constellation of Virgo is visible between latitudes 80 degrees and -80 degrees and is best seen in the month of May around 9 PM in the Northern Hemisphere.

Virgo is filled with exoplanets.

There are 35 verified exoplanets orbiting 29 stars in Virgo.

One of the stars in the constellation, 70 Virginis, contains **one of the first discovered extrasolar planetary systems**.

The size of Virgo not only applies to its breadth in the heavens, but also to the size of some of its planets. One of the confirmed planets in Virgo is 7.5 times the mass of Jupiter.

And another star in Virgo, Chi Virginis, has one of the most massive planets ever detected, at a mass of 11.1 times that of Jupiter.

Another star in the constellation, 61 Virginis, has 3 orbiting planets that we are aware of, but scientists suspect there may be more. One of the planets orbiting 61 Virginis is a super earth and is equivalent in size to our planet Neptune.

A "super earth" is a planet with more mass than Earth, but with less mass than a larger planet in our solar system like Uranus or Neptune.

Super earths can be made of rock and metal or even ice and gas. They can have atmospheres with oceans, or they can contain nothing but hydrogen and helium. For our species to settle on a super earth in another location, we would need a similar sized planet but also one that has a great deal of rock intis makeup and one that is located in what scientists call the habitable zone. This is the region where the planets are the right distance from the star they orbit for liquid water to be present.

A bit more on Spica and the other brightest stars in Virgo.

Spica, also known by the Latin name *Alpha Virginis*, is the brightest star in the constellation of Virgo. It is a nearly perfect example of a star of the first magnitude.

Spica is a blue giant about 260 light-years from Earth is about twice as big as the Sun. And its luminosity is 2,300 times that of our Sun. Spica still is often referred to as the "ear of wheat" held by the maiden.

The second brightest star in Virgo is **Porrima** (also called *Arich* and *Gamma Virginis*), which is actually a binary star.

The third brightest star in the constellation is a yellow giant named **Vindemiatrix**, "the grape gatherer." It is also referred to as *Epsilon Virginis*, based on magnitude.

Other findings of significance in Virgo.

Eleven deep space objects cataloged by Charles Messier are found in the Virgo constellation. This is more deep space objects than in any constellation other than Sagittarius, which has fifteen.

Virgo is also the home to the Quasar 3C 273, which was the first Quasar ever to be identified. With the magnitude of 12.9 it also is optically the brightest Quasar in the sky.

The first exoplanets ever found were found in 1994 in the constellation of Virgo.

These exoplanets were found around the Pulsar star referred to as PSR B1257+12.

A Pulsar like this star is a type of neutron star formed after a massive supernova of a star exploding then collapsing. Pulsars are characterized by extremely rapid rotation.

In 2009, three planets orbiting the star 61 Virginis were discovered by astronomers. Each is considered a super-earth due to masses ranging between the mass of Earth and the mass of Neptune. One is classified as having five times the mass of Earth, another 16 times the mass of Earth, and still another 118 times the mass of Earth. These are not small planets circling 61 Virginis.

Galaxy clusters & black holes in Virgo.

The constellation of Virgo also possesses several galaxy clusters that are located in what is called the Sombrero Galaxy.

The Sombrero Galaxy is about 28 million light-years from Earth. It is an amazingly brilliant white and almost flat galaxy with a bulbous core encircled by thick dust of a spiral galaxy. Scientists postulate the center of the Sombrero Galaxy is a massive black hole based on observations of X-ray emissions that suggest material is falling into the compact core.

The Sombrero Galaxy contains nearly 2,000 globular clusters — which is 10 times more than the number of globular clusters in our Milky Way Galaxy. It appears the age of the Sombrero is close to the age of our Milky Way, ranging from 10 billion to 13 billion years old. It has an apparent magnitude of 8 and is beyond the limit of normal eyesight without use of a telescope. But aided, it can be seen best in May. The galaxy has a mass that equals 800 billion of our Suns and is one of the most massive objects in the Virgo galaxy cluster—which should indicate the constellation of Virgo is not a stranger to huge objects within its bounds, at least within the bounds of Virgo as viewed from Earth.

The Sombrero Galaxy was discovered by one of Charles Messier's colleagues, French astronomer and comet hunter Pierre Méchain, in 1781. But most of the detailed information we have learned about it has come from observations through the Hubble Telescope that was launched into space aboard the Space Shuttle Discovery in 1990 and continuing research on the data it provides NASA and the Hubble Heritage Team.

New insights into the meaning of Virgo?

It is interesting to note the **decidedly feminine mystique** attached to the constellation of Virgo across cultures and times.

One can't help but pause on the **deeply womanly** and **feminine** concept of Virgo in the Babylonian mind—**food and nourishment** on one hand, and shade, the **sweetness** of dates, and the life-saving gift of **water** on the other. The simple Ear of Grain and the Palm Frond. The two essences of Life. Food and Water.

Even the later Greeks saw the **innocent lushness** and **fertility** of Virgo as well as the **passive strength** of the goddess Demeter.

These concepts seem foreign to more modern depictions of critical thought and pickiness and the cold or barren energy many see as Virgo today. The lushness of nature seems to have given way to a clinical scrubbing somewhere across the centuries.

Even the **rich and bountiful sustenance** seen by the ancients has today become more seen as *diet*—a concept most modern people see as restrictive rather than a sign of plenitude and bounty.

Perhaps it was the **superimposition of the Virgin Mary onto the fertility of youth** that was the major pivot. It is difficult to say. But certainly replacement of ancient mythology with an overlay of Christian symbolism was not uncommon.

Early Christianity tried to stamp out as many "pagan" thoughts and beliefs as possible. And likely nowhere was there more fervor to do so than anything concerned with the blessed Virgin. Once that substitution of the Blessed Virgin Mary was made, it not only seemed to stick like glue, but it seems to have almost totally erased the older meanings of all of the plethora of goddesses associated with the sign in antiquity.

We know scientifically there is a **huge black hole** in Virgo. And it does indeed appear that much was lost through it.

But—we also know scientifically that Virgo is huge. And not only is it huge in that it takes up a really large portion of our visible sky, we know today that it has vast clusters of stars within it—enough stars and stars systems to almost literally stun the mind. There is, without a single breath of a doubt, far more to be discovered.

After all, Virgo has shown itself to a constellation of firsts.

The first exoplanets were found in Virgo. The first quasar was discovered in Virgo. One of first extra-solar planetary systems ever found is in Virgo. The first black hole ever seen is in Virgo. And with all of the super earths we today know are in Virgo, perhaps the first habitable planet for man . . . .

THE

CONSTELLATION OF

LIBRA

How Libra was seen in antiquity.

In the Babylonian calendar Libra was considered the "Month of the Sun."

Since Libra today is where the Autumnal Equinox occurs, that concept is a bit of a head-scratcher for us. The Autumnal Equinox is one of the moments in our solar year that the days and nights are of equal length. But immediately after the Autumnal Equinox, the hours of darkness each day become increasingly more and the hours of sunlight are increasingly fewer.

So, assuming the sky was pretty much in the same place it is right now (which really means, of course, that Earth is), the "Month of the Sun" was really something like the "Month of Goodbye to the Sun." We can only assume it was in that vein the Babylonians saw it.

In Greek mythology, Libra was related to the Goddess of Divine Justice Themis and her six daughters, who comprised The Horai and the Moirai; the Goddess of The Balancing of Equal Weights Atalanta; and the Goddess of Human Justice Astraea.

We clearly see a repeating pattern here although the original Greek words have difference nuances and shadings when it comes to the meaning of Libra.

But there were still more goddesses than these interwoven with Libra throughout history. It is a sign that was filled with feminine energy in ancient legends.

And oddly, much as the rib of the man Adam was taken to make the woman Eve, the Scales of Justice were taken out of the constellation of Virgo to make part of the constellation of Libra.

But to understand the most ancient concepts of Libra, we must look to Themis and her daughters as well as to Astraea and Atalanta.

Themis.

Themis may be the most richly illuminating of the three in terms of understanding the ancient layers of meaning underlying the sign of Libra.

Themis was the Goddess of Divine Law—
the traditional rules of order, custom, and
conduct established by the gods.

She also was a prophetic goddess who
presided over the most ancient oracles,
including Delphoi (the Delphi Oracles). In
this role, she was the divine voice (themistes)
who first instructed mankind in the primal
laws of justice and morality, such as piety,
hospitality, good governance, assembly, and
pious offerings to the gods. In Greek, the
word themis referred to Divine Law, those
rules of conduct long established by custom.
Her domain was not that of human decree,
but rather Heavenly Law. She was closely
identified with Demeter Thesmophoros, the
"Bringer of Law."

The daughter of Uranus and Gaea, Themis
was an early bride of Zeus and she was his
first counselor. She was often depicted as
sitting next to Zeus's throne advising him on
Divine Law and the Rules of Fate. In a very
real way, she was the bridge between Zeus
and the Divine since she was seen as the
voice of the Divine.

But here is where the legends about
Themis get really interesting. Themis had six
children, all daughters.

Three of Themis's daughters were called
the Horai, the Goddesses of the Seasons and
the Keepers of the Gates of Heaven.

And the other of her three daughters were called the Moirai, or The Fates, the Goddesses of the Inescapable Destiny of Man.

The Horai.

Three of Themis's daughters collectively were called The Horai.

They were called the "Goddesses of the Seasons," but in reality were tied only to one season—Spring.

It is possible this wasn't some sort of weird mistake or sloppy linguistics, but rather that the ancient Greeks saw Spring as the beginning of the cycle of seasons. And thus, Spring was viewed as the "birth" of all of the seasons.

However, it remains curious that goddesses appearing in the constellation of Libra were associated with Spring since today's Western Zodiac considers Libra an autumnal house and the location of the Sun at the Autumnal equinox, not the Vernal (or Spring) Equinox.

This fact gives us dessert for some modern pondering—because remember the Babylonians who preceded the Greeks called Libra the "Month of the Sun."

Nonetheless, The Horai were closely associated with Spring in the ancient Greek mind, while The Horai in the heavens were viewed, and remain viewable, in the sign of Libra.

One of The Horai was Eumonia, the "Goddess of Good Order and Lawful Conduct," who ruled over good and just laws and civil order. She was often associated with the role of the dutiful and proper married woman. Eumonia's dominion of Spring was the springtime of green pastures.

Dike, another of The Horai, was the "Goddess of Justice and Fair Judgments." She had dominion over the rights established by custom and law. Some say Dike may have been the first example of a "common-law" wife. Her aspect of Spring was the springing of earned new growth.

And Eirene, the "Goddess of Peaceful and Calm Spring," was the goddesses who encouraged thinking before going to war and reminded Greeks that peace holds great bounty. Interestingly, late spring was the typical time for Greeks to begin their campaigns to conquer new lands or to go to war, so the Goddess of a Peaceful Spring had deeply significant meaning in terms of pacifism and the value of calm family life. Eirene is often depicted holding a baby, Ploutous, the "God of Wealth." Eirene's aspect of springtime is seen in the abundant wealth that peaceful calm brings.

The Moirai.

Themis's other three daughters were called The Moirai. They ruled the dominion of the Inescapable Destiny of Man. Clearly, this is a great insight into ancient thought.

Mankind has Seasons of Life (The Horai).
But Mankind also has Inescapable Destiny (The Moirai).

The Greek word moirai means "parts," "shares," or "allotted portions." The role of the Moirai was to assign every living being his or her Fate or share in the overall scheme of things.

Themis's three daughters who comprised the Moirai were **Klotho** (sometimes spelled Clotho), **Lakhesis** (or Lachesis), and **Atropos** (sometimes appearing as Aisa). They were known as "The Spinner of the Thread of Life," "The Apportioner of Lots," and "She Who Cannot Be Turned." All three were aspects of and under the direction of Zeus Moriagetes, The God of Fate.

At the birth of each human, the Moirai spun the thread of that particular being's life, and then they followed his or her steps throughout the lifetime, directing the consequences of the person's actions in accordance with the will of the gods.

The fate of a human was not seen as set in stone.

Zeus had great latitude and power to alter the course of a human's life and even to save a person already at the point of being walloped by his fate. The Moirai never abruptly and directly interceded in a person's life, but served as intermediaries to mitigate consequences of actions. The lots or destinies that were assigned to mortals were seldom absolutes. Rather they were **conditional destinies**. Men were seen as having the freedom to exercise a certain influence on their individual fates by purity of soul and by decisions made and actions taken in life.

And since man's fate was seen as culminating and ending at his death, the **Goddesses of Fate** were also considered the **Goddesses of Death**, or the *Moirai Thanatoio*.

But the Moirai were more than simply worker bees for the gods. They worked independently, they directed fate, and they kept a watchful eye over the fate assigned to every being to ensure that eternal laws would be obeyed in human evolution.

Mankind—as well as Zeus and all the other gods—had to submit to the Moirai.

The Moirai often were depicted as ugly old women, sometimes lame or disfigured. They were seen as severe, harsh, and inflexible despite the fluid nature of Fate itself.

Klotho usually was seen carrying a spindle or a roll, the one with which she spun the thread of each person's life just prior to birth. She was referred to as **"The Spinner."** This probably is the genesis of our modern word "cloth."

Lakhesis was typically depicted carrying a staff with which she points to a horoscope on a globe. Thus, she may have had an intimate connection with early astrology. Her typical name was the **"Apportioner of Lots,"** as in the lots of life.

And ***Atropos***, the one they called **"She Who Cannot Be Turned,"** was usually characterized as carrying a scroll or wax tablet, or sometimes holding a sundial or a scales or some type of cutting instrument like "The Knife of Discrimination."

Often the three goddesses of the Moirai were depicted together. And in those renderings, the Moirai were typically seen with crowns or scepters or staffs, symbols of dominion and rulership.

153

And during this time, we find that the Moirai appear in many depictions of a person's birth. In these drawings, the Moirai are shown spinning, measuring, and cutting the thread of life.

The Moirai later appear in a highly similar form in Roman mythology. But the Moirai were called the *Parcae* by the Romans. And the three goddesses names were *Nona* (instead of Klotho), *Decuma* (instead of Lakhesis), and *Morta* (instead of Atropos).

Atalanta.

As rich as Themis and her daughters are in adding to our understanding Libra, it is not complete without learning about Atalanta and her connection to the constellation of Libra.

Atalanta was a great huntress, a skilled archer, and a favorite of the goddess Artemis. But she had a really difficult early life.

Atalanta was abandoned as a baby by her father in the wilds of the woods. Some say it was because he only wanted a son. But, regardless of the reason, legend says she was found by a mother bear who took her as her own and suckled her so she would not die. Then as a child, hunters found her in the woods and raised her.

The name Atalanta comes from the Greek word atalantos, meaning "equal in weight."

According to legend, Atalanta swore herself to virginity early in life. And one day, while she was out hunting, two Kentauroi (Centaurs) suddenly appeared in the grove where she was hunting and attempted to molest her. She killed both of them with arrows.

She lived as an adventuress and warrior. In fact, according to Greek legend, she joined Jason and the Argonauts on their voyage. And she defeated the hero Peleus in a wrestling match during the funeral games of King Pelias.

And when King Oineus (sometimes referred to as Oeneus) summoned heroes to destroy the Kalydonian Boar, Atalanta not only answered his call to slay the boar, but she was the first hunter to draw blood in the hunt.

As the legend continues, Atalanta was awarded the boar's skin as the prize of the hunt, as was the custom for the hunter who drew first blood. But her uncles took offense that a woman should win, and they attempted to take the skin from her by force. Atalanta single-handedly killed them all in the ensuing skirmish. She walked away with the boar's skin.

Other legends say that Atalanta was finally reunited with her father, and he insisted that she wed. She agreed to marriage on the condition that any suitor must race her and that all losers be put to death; she agreed only to marry the man who could best her in the race.

All-or-nothing.

According to this legend, the lad Melanion (sometimes called by the name of Hippomenes) asked the goddess Aphrodite for help to win the race. Aphrodite, who always favored love and coupling, gave Melanion three magical golden apples and told him to throw each of them in front of Atalanta at different times during the race. And so Melanion challenged Atalanta to a race, threw out the apples as directed by Aphrodite, and each time Atalanta stooped to retrieve an apple, she was slowed down just enough for Melanion to win both the race and Atalanta's hand in marriage.

However, unfortunately for Melanion, he deluded himself into believing it was his strength and charm, not the golden apples, that had won the race and Atalanta's heart. So Melanion refused to pay Aphrodite her due. Aphrodite then cursed Melanion and, under the curse, he was induced to lie with his wife in the sacred hall of Zeus, which caused the offended deity to banish both

Melanion and Atalanta from the earthly plane by transforming both of them into lions for eternity.

On one hand, Atalanta seems intimately entwined with the dictates of unequal gender "roles" and a strong woman who demanded gender equality in a time it was given reluctantly if ever given. And, on the other hand, in what seems to be a totally reversed role from Hebraic Adam & Eve legend, it was a man who was the temptation and the final downfall of Atalanta.

Astraea.

Astraea (sometimes spelled Astraia) was seen as the Virgin Goddess of Justice.

During the Golden Age of Greece, legend says that Astraea lived on Earth with mankind. But as the Bronze Age ushered in increased lawlessness and debauchery among mortals, Astraea rejected this kind of debased behavior and chose to leave the Earth. Zeus honored her by setting her in the sky as the constellation of Virgo.

You notice that, right? Not as Libra. As Virgo. In Greek mythology Astraea was placed in the constellation of Virgo. The constellation of Libra had not yet been separated from Virgo. That separation did not happen until Roman times. Astraea was placed in the part of the heavens that was Virgo but became Libra when the Romans re-divided the sky and the constellations.

The name Astraea literally means "well balanced."

Astraea is sometimes depicted as holding lightning and standing beside the throne of Zeus. She is drawn as a star-goddess, with wings, a flaming torch, and a glowing aureole, or halo, around her head.

In a thought-provoking twist, Astraea is usually the goddess who was depicted as holding the Scales of Justice in the Greek World, though she may have been used somewhat interchangeably with her mother, Themis. Historians differ on that point. But when Astraea went up to heaven and became the constellation of Virgo, she took the Scales of Justice with her.

So the Scales of Justice originally were found in Virgo, not in Libra. The Scales of Justice became associated with Libra only after the Romans re-drew the sky and created the constellation Libra.

Many of the ancient legends hold a prophecy of a Golden Age that will someday come again. According to this prophecy, the Golden Age will be heralded by Astraea's return to Earth to again walk among humans.

Other Goddesses Associated with Libra.

Libra is also related to the Greco Roman goddess Aphrodite/Venus. And sometimes it also is associated with the goddesses Eris/Discorida, Hermione/Concordia, Hera/Juno, Ishtar, Freyja and Frigg, and the god Xolotl.

No other sign of the zodiac seems to have direct connections with as wide a panoply of goddesses (and to a far lesser extent gods) as Libra, although Virgo comes close.

Much like in the constellation of Virgo, the prevailing theme of Libra in antiquity seems to be the form of a female deity.

The Indian version of Libra is Tula, and the Chinese version of Libra is the Dragon.

One interesting correlation is that Libra is the only intimate object used as a Zodiac symbol in the modern Western zodiac. And in the Chinese zodiac the equivalent of Libra is the Dragon, the only mythological creature in the Chinese zodiac. So in both on both sides of the world, the sign of Libra has been considered an anomaly, a type unto itself, unique since our earliest beginnings.

A Specific Note about the "New" Constellation of Libra.

When we say "new," we have to keep in mind that all things are relative.

Approximately 3,500 years ago, the Romans re-drew the sky map to "create" the Libra constellation. At that time, the constellation of Libra contained the Autumnal Equinox—the dividing line in the visual sky where the sun crosses the equator along it's apparent journey from the Northern Hemisphere to the Southern Hemisphere. It is at that moment, twice each year (once at the Autumnal Equinox and once at the Vernal Equinox), when Earth's days and nights are of equal length.

Some say it is because of that placement of the Autumnal Equinox that seemed to "balance" days and nights to equality that the scales were chosen for the symbol for Libra.

From the mythological history involving Libra, that idea is probably only partially true. But the glyph we use for the sign today does seems to reflect that concept.

Keep in mind Libra is a hybrid constellation historically. Part of Virgo was "taken" and part of Scorpio was "taken" to create it.

While in almost all ways the astrology, and even much of the mythology, of ancient Greece was taken by the Romans and simply renamed from the Greek words to the Roman words, the constellation of Libra is Roman.

But, of course, we know from Babylonian records that what is deemed a constellation and what is used as a sign in the astrological wheel has always been fluid.

The Apparently Forgotten Contribution of Scorpio to the Constellation of Libra.

Lest you leaving thinking only Virgo went into the making of Libra, Scorpio was robbed as well. When the Romans remapped the constellations about 3,500 years ago, they took the two claws of the "Creature with the Burning Sting" out of Scorpius to serve as the arms of the scales.

And, in fact, the earliest Roman sources do not use the word Libra in reference to the newly added constellation. The great Roman poet Aratus and a host of other classical writers refer to the new constellation as "The Claws" of Scorpius. It was only through popular reference over the ensuing centuries that the old Greek name of Libra was used for the new constellation.

And one other interesting note about the name is that the original Greek word was "LY bruh," with a long 'i.' It was the Romans who called it by the Roman pronunciation of "LEE bruh."

And, inching closer to modern times...

As seen in the 17th century by William Ramesey in his astrological treatise Astrologia Restaurata:

> *The seventh sign is called Libra (signifying Balance) for that the Sun being therein, both the length of the days and nights, as also the temper of the ayr, are in balance. As it were neither inclining one way nor other; the days and nights being of an equal length through the whole World; and the temperature of the ayr between the decayed heat of Summer, and the approaching cold of winter, is neither tending one way or other, but as it were in a balance.*

What we know about the constellation of Libra today.

First cataloged by Ptolemy in the 2nd century, Libra is a relatively faint constellation but is not impossible to view with the naked eye depending on light and weather conditions.

It has no first magnitude stars.

The constellation of Libra ranks twenty-ninth overall in terms of size of constellations and covers 538 square degrees of sky.

Libra is located in the southern hemisphere between Scorpio to the east and Virgo to the West. In addition to Scorpio and

Virgo, Libra borders Serpens Caput, Hydra, Centaurus, Lupus, and Ophiuchus.

Libra is visible in the sky between 65 degrees and -90 degrees, and is best seen in the Northern Hemisphere during the month of June around 9 PM.

The three brightest stars in Libra are **Zubeneschamali** and **Zubenelgenubi**, and **Zubenelhakrabi**—which together make up the upper portion of the scales that links the two balances, hanging off the triangle at an angle.

The brightest star in the constellation is **Zubeneschamali** (or Beta Librae), a blue dwarf with the magnitude of 2.7 located 160 light-years from Earth. This star is **the only star to appear green** to the naked eye. It is often also called "The Northern Claw" or sometimes "The Northern Scales."

The second brightest star in Libra is **Zubenelgenubi** (or Alpha Librae), a double star 77 light-years away that is intrinsically more luminous than our Sun. Until very recently scientists thought *Zubenelgenubi* was a binary star, two physically related stars orbiting a common center of mass. But most astronomers today hypothesize it is actually the brighter of a double star. *Zubenelgenubi* is also called "The Southern Claw."

Where did the names of claws come from? Both *Zubenelgenubi* and its more northern companion *Zubeneschamali* were originally perceived by the Babylonians and the Greeks as being in the constellation of Scorpius, or Scorpio. Combined, "The Claws," originally referenced the two claws of "The Creature with the Burning Sting" that was the centerpiece of the constellation of Scorpius.

Remember, the constellation of Libra did not exist during the time of the Babylonians or ancient Greeks.

Another of the brighter stars in Libra (relative to the dimness of the constellation) is **Zubenelhakrabi** (or Gamma Librae), an orange giant with a magnitude of 3.9 that is suspected to be a binary star. *Zubenelhakrabi* is located between 152 and 163 light-years from Earth. It has a radius more than 11 times larger than our Sun and shines 72 times as brightly as our Sun. *Zubenelhakrabi* also was originally conceived as part of The Claws of Scorpius.

The oldest star in the universe is located in Libra.

One truly significant note about Libra is that it is home to the oldest known star in the universe: Methuselah.

Named after the man referred to in the book of Genesis in the Old Testament of the Bible as the oldest man who ever lived, until recently Methuselah has been estimated to be 16 billion years old. But with recent data from the Hubble Telescope, scientists estimate it is more likely 14.5 billion years old, plus or minus 0.8 billion.

Probably born in a dwarf galaxy that was cannibalized by the Milky Way more than 12 billion years ago, Methuselah dates back to the very origins of the Universe. In fact, in an apparent Cosmic riddle, scientists tell us that **Methuselah appears to pre-date the universe**.

Methuselah is about twice the size of Jupiter and orbits around two stars, making it an unusual circumbinary planet that is 190.1 light-years from Earth. It appears to be in the very early stages of expansion into a red giant. Right now it is a 7th magnitude star, and with a good pair of amateur binoculars is visible on a clear night.

Another note of significance about the constellation of Libra is that the discovery of the first potentially habitable planet, or "super earth," was found there.

Today we know that within Libra is a planetary system named Gliese 581 that has several planets, two of which our scientists classify as super earths—or planets orbiting close enough to their stars that there is possibility of liquid water on the surface of the planet. One of these planets, Gliese 581 c, has a mass 5 times that of the Earth. And the other, Gliese 581 d, has a mass 7.7 times the mass of our Earth. Gliese 581 d is on the cold side of the zone, so it may be a less hospitable host to life as we know it. At this point, we have made no physical probes of either of these planets in Gliese 581, so it remains conjecture.

New insights into the meaning of Libra?

L ibra is unique in the modern astrological zodiac for two reasons.

First, is it the "new" constellation. And it appears that in Libra, astrology may have led astronomy. We find no records of *why* this change occurred in the astrological zodiac, only that it did.

And second, Libra is the only Zodiac constellation that has an inanimate symbol— being neither animal, mythological creature, nor human—but rather a "thing." No other Zodiac Constellation centers on the inanimate.

In its most fundamental form, Libra seems to be *conceptual* at the heart of its character—the sign of *ideals* that humans strive for. And possibly for ideals that humans find the most difficult to master or to attain.

Like **Balance**. And **Social Justice**. And **Equality of the Sexes**. And **Peace**. And **Calm**.

Living in accord with **Divine Law**. Humans have a difficult time even agreeing on what Divine Law *is*, let alone living in accordance with it.

But it seems the ancients may have been attempting to lay out their concept of Divine Law in all of the old myths we associate with Libra. We just conveniently forgot them.

It bears note that **only a goddess** is connected to the Scales of Justice. She seems to be the only one who ever really used the scales, though she always held them up for mankind.

Astraea herself was never the symbol for Libra. She only recognized and utilized the symbol.

Even if mankind did not.

And after Astraea gave up on humanity and took the scales with her to the sky, she continues to hold it there for all to see, and to strive for.

Remember the ancient prophecy is that humans will someday grow enough to grasp the concepts of **Justice** and **Peace** and **Equality** and the goddess Astraea will return to Earth with the scales and walk among us again.

There is not one single astrological myth other that the one connected with Libra where a deity took the essence of a sign from the Earth. Nor is there a single other myth that contains this kind of promise or prophecy of a future Golden Age.

The sign of Libra is indeed unique. And special.

Another of the most curious things about the mythology connected with Libra is that although humans were seen in antiquity as each being given a specific fate, they each also had the freedom to exercise influence their given fate by purity of soul, by decisions made, and actions taken in life. We see this concept today very clearly in the practice of Vedic Astrology and the "prescriptions" Vedic astrologers often give. But the concept has been almost totally lost in Western astrology.

But one of the most truly remarkable parts of the lost Libra mythology is its explicit connection with VIRGINITY.

Although the Christianizing of the constellation of Virgo more or less whitewashed Virgo into an association with the Virgin Mary, in antiquity there was no record of "virginity" per se in the Virgo legends. Innocent and youth, yes. But *fertile* innocence and youth, not a negation of sexuality or even a refusal of sexual activity.

Yet in the Atalanta myth associated with **Libra**, Atalanta did pledge herself to virginity early in life. In the ancient mind, virginity was expressly part of Libra, not Virgo.

But more than that, **virginity was tied to female empowerment**.

It was *Atalanta's choice* to remain a virgin.

Virginity was not superimposed on her by a society or a religion or even by morality. It was a *choice*. HER choice.

And when males attempted to negate Atalanta's decision and take Atalanta by force, she had the power and strength to fight them to the death. She won.

And when she finally agreed to take a husband, it had to be on *her* terms.

Although the Libra mythology is riddled with gender inequality, it also was integrally tied to righting the imbalance.

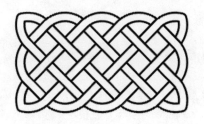

THE

CONSTELLATION OF

SCORPIO

How Scorpio was seen

in antiquity.

T he Latin name for Scorpio is literally translated as "creature with the burning sting."

However Scorpius is not seen as a scorpion by everyone. And even in Western Astrology, the earliest concepts may not have been a scorpion as we understand them today.

Modern Javanese people of Indonesia call this constellation Bangyakangrem ("the brooded swan") or Kalapa Doyong ("the leaning coconut tree").

In Hawaii, Scorpio is known as the demigod Maui's "Fishhook."

In Chinese mythology, the constellation of Scorpio was traditionally part of the **Azure**

Dragon. It is the Azure Dragon that appears as the **guardian god at the entrances of Taoist temples**. The Azure Dragon appeared on the Chinese national flag from 1862-1912 and as one of the twelve symbols on the national emblem of China from 1913-1928, although today it no longer appears as an "official" protector of China. The Azure Dragon remains, however, embedded in Chinese mysticism. In ancient China the dragon, and most particularly the Azure Dragon, was considered a sign of **supreme good luck**. In Taoism it is viewed as representing the **highest state of the human spiri**t. And in Chinese Feng Shui, the Azure Dragon is often used as a cure or augmentation connected to the family space, the kitchen, or the home office. To Chinese Feng Shui practitioners, a misplaced or poorly placed dragon does more harm than good because it **devolves to a lowly snake when incorrectly used**. In Chinese symbolism, the dragon has no wings, yet it can fly. It often lives in or near water. And it is the source of **tremendous life energy** and **blessings**.

The Azure Dragon appears in Japanese mythology as well, although in a slightly different shade of blue and with slightly different natural "homes." In Japan, the Azure Dragon is called the **Bluegreen Dragon**, and is considered one of the five guardian spirits of cities. Kyoto seems to be the epicenter of this belief. It is considered that the Bluegreen Dragon guards the city of Kyoto from the East, the Black Tortoise from the North, the White Tiger from the West, the Vermilion Bird from the South, and the Yellow Dragon from the Center. In the city of Kyoto, temples stand even today dedicated to each of these gods. The gate of the Kiyomizu Temple in eastern Kyoto is guarded by a statue of the Bluegreen Dragon who is believed to drink from a waterfall within the temple complex every night when no mortals are present. In 1983, archaeologists found depictions of the Bluegreen Dragon and the other directional gods at the Kitora Tomb at Asuka, the most ancient evidence we have of the deification of these gods in Japanese antiquity.

In the East, the dragons were seen as the **Giver of Life** and **Abundance**.

Not so much so in the West where dragons were considered **something to be greatly feared**. And, ultimately, **to be conquered**.

In some ancient Western texts, Scorpio was associated not with a scorpion, but with either a mystical bird or a mystical dragon.

Taking into consideration some of the most ancient texts and creation stories in the West, the "creature with a burning sting" may have originated not from the stinger of a

175

scorpion, but rather from a more encompassing sting of a fire-breathing winged dragon. And in many of the most ancient legends, these winged dragon creatures not only breathed fire and could fly, but they also could swim. They were believed to be at home in the sea, able to suddenly emerge upon land, and able to rapidly descend upon humans from the sky and then disappear by flying way back out to sea to dive deep beneath the waters of the ocean.

It may be through myths of the dragon as a creature of the sea that Scorpio is associated with a water sign.

Some Gaelic antiquarians believe this ancient dragon myth is the source of legends such as the Loch Ness Monster as well as the plethora of European myths of knights as dragon slayers.

Then in some more recent Western texts, the Scorpio dragon idea seems to have morphed into the Phoenix, a mythological bird whose dead body bursts into flames, disintegrates into a pile of ashes, then unexpectedly rises whole from the ashes to fly above the earth. The Phoenix: he who cannot be killed. The Phoenix is master of Life and Death. Or master of Life **through** Death.

Although Scorpio is a water sign, the complexity of the sign in antiquity is clear.

To the 17th century mind, Scorpio was described in the Astrologia Restaurata by William Ramesey:

> *The eighth is called Scorpio (signifying a Scorpion) because when the Sun is therein, cold and dryness is predominate, which are obnoxious to nature, and by reason the natural temper of the ayr is hot and moyst; the ayr is thereby corrupted, so that dangerous diseases are ingendred thereby, as pestilential Feavers, Plagues and the like.*

From the preceding paragraph, one might intuit Ramesey did not much care for the sign of Scorpio.

Knowing what we know today about the many unusually complex star systems and anomalies within the area of the sky we know as Scorpio, it is fascinating to look back on how humans have viewed the symbolism over time and cultures. Somehow mankind always knew Scorpio was intricately complicated, even before our modern space exploration showed   us.

What we know about the constellation of Scorpio today.

The constellation of Scorpio, technically the constellation of *Scorpius* (the Latin name), is one of the brightest constellations in the sky.

The 33rd largest constellation, Scorpio occupies 497 square degrees of the sky. It is situated in the third quadrant of the Southern Hemisphere, high in the sky near the center of the Milky Way. In the Southern Hemisphere, it is visible between latitudes +40 degrees and -90 degrees. In the Northern Hemisphere, Scorpio lies close to the southern horizon and is best seen in the month of July around 9 PM.

The constellation of Scorpio used to be larger. Up until Roman times, the constellation of Scorpio contained "The Claws" of the "Creature with the Burning Sting," what we today call the scorpion. When the Romans re-classified the sky about 3,500 years ago, they took part of Scorpio and part of Virgo to create the "new" constellation of Libra.

Scorpio contains a large number of planets that are potentially habitable by humans.

Scorpios houses a collection of curious and widely varying exoplanets that range from being extremely old in age to being quite new and even potentially habitable.

In fact, Scorpio has 13 stars with known planets.

One of the planets found in Scorpio is a super earth named Gliese 667Cc that is approximately four times the size of Earth. It orbits a red dwarf star called Gliese 667C, a star that is part of a three-star system only 22 light-years from Earth. This planet is potentially habitable.

That same system within the Scorpio constellation contains two other potentially habitable planets: Gliese 667Ce and Gliese 667Cf, both about 2.7 times the size of Earth.

It is important to note that at the current time our astronomers define "habitability" as a rocky world that is close enough to its parent star that liquid water might exist on the surface.

There are, however, other factors that come into play for habitability. The composition of a planet's atmosphere and the long-term viability of the host star are two of the most important factors.

Scorpio is full of bright stars.

The constellation of Scorpio has an exceptional number of unusually bright stars, including *Antares, Graffias, Dschubba, Sargas, Shaula, Jabbah, Girtab, Iclil, Al Niyat* (a name shared by two stars) and *Lesath*. Several of the stars in Scorpio are binary stars and a surprisingly large number are **complex multiple star systems**.

ANTARES.

Probably the most well-known of the stars in Scorpio is **Antares**, which is also called Alpha Scorpii. *Antares* has been known by different names in various cultures over time.

180

The Babylonians called it as GABA
GIR.TAB, "The Breast of the Scorpion." The
Egyptians called it Serket, the scorpion
goddess. And the Persians knew it as Satevis,
one of the four "Royal Stars." But in all these
cultures Antares was both known and given
great importance.

Antares is one of four first magnitude stars
lying within 5 degrees of the ecliptic:
Aldebaran in Taurus, Spica in Virgo, Regulus
in Leo, and Antares in Scorpio. That is likely
why these stars played such a huge role in the
ancient world. They were heavily relied upon
for navigation, thus they were referred to in
antiquity as the four "Royal Stars."

Antares can be occulted by the Moon, and
less often it can be occulted by Venus. The
last recorded occultation of Antares by Venus
happened on September 17, 525 BC.—so it is
quite rare, although it physically can happen.

A red supergiant star, Antares has a radius
approximately 883 times that of our Sun and
is roughly 10,000 times more luminous. It is
estimated to be about 12 million years old,
compared to our Sun that is estimated to be
4.6 billion years old.

As far back as ancient Babylonia, Antares
was compared to the planet Mars, probably
due to its brightness and its red appearance.

Antares is the brightest star in modern
Scorpio and the sixteenth brightest star in the
sky with an apparent magnitude between
0.96 and 1.8. It is part of a **binary system**
with the faint companion named **Shaula** (or

Lambda Scorpii), the second brightest star in the constellation and the twenty-fifth brightest star in the sky with an apparent magnitude of approximately 1.63. Modern astronomers have confirmed that Shaula (in Arabic "the raised tail") also is made of two stars, and possibly a third, based on the number of unexpected x-rays it produces.

Antares is actually an unusual type of multiple star system even though it is classified as a binary system.

Antares is considered to be located "at the heart of the scorpion." Its companion Shaula is located at the scorpion's tail.

The other major stars in Scorpio.

Graffias (or Acrab, Akrab, Elacrab, or Beta Scorpii) appears as a binary star through a small telescope, but actually is another multiple star system. We know today that both of the stars in the binary contain at least 10 solar masses each, so the system is quite large and complex. Each is expected to end their lifespans as massive Type II supernova explosions.

Deschubba (Iclarcrau, Iclarkrav, or Delta Scorpii) is also a multiple star system. It has two companion stars, both with decidedly irregular orbits. In Arabic the name Descubba means "the forehead," referring to its location in the forehead of the scorpion.

Sargas (Theta Scorpii) has at least one companion star. It is a star that has been known since earliest antiquity, still bearing the name given to it by the Sumerians, although the meaning of its name has been lost. Today we know it is an evolved bright yellow giant with a radius 26 times that of our Sun and a luminosity 1,834 greater. It has an apparent magnitude of 1.87 and is approximately 300 light-years from our solar system.

Jabbah (also Nu Scorpii or 14 Scorpii) is another multiple star system in the constellation of Scorpio. It is located approximately 437 light years from Earth and composed of two close groups of stars separated by only 41 seconds of arc. The brighter group contains two subgiants, and the fainter group contains two main sequence dwarf stars. Jabba illuminates the reflection of the nearby "Blue Horse Head Nebula" (IC 4592) that appears to gaze towards Orion.

Girtab (Xi Scorpii) is still another multiple star system in Scorpio. It contains at least five stars forming two groups that are separated by 4.67 arc minutes. The larger group is comprised of two yellow-white stars and at least one companion star, with visual magnitudes of 4.8, 5.1, and 7.6. The second group is comprised of two Class K stars that may have a companion star. Scientists say there appears to be a sixth star in Girtab, but a definite gravitational tie to any of the other stars has not been confirmed.

Iclil (Pi Scorpii) is a triple star system with a combined visual magnitude of 2.9. Approximately 590 light-years from Earth. Iclil contains an eclipsing binary star and has a wide variation in brightness because of intersecting orbits with other stars in the system that periodically mutually block each other's light. Two of the stars in the Iclil system are hot sequence stars that are rapid rotators with extremely close proximities to each other. The third star in the system is a distant companion with on a 12.2 visual magnitude. The primary star of the Iclil system is 21,900 times more luminous than our Sun and has approximately 12-13 solar masses.

Lesath (Upsilon Scorpii) is a single subgiant star with the visual magnitude of 2.7 that is located 580 light-years from Earth. Lesath is 11 times the mass of our Sun and 12,300 times brighter. It's Arabic name comes from the word las'a, meaning "the pass (or the bite) of a poisonous animal." And, not too surprisingly, it is located in the scorpion's stinger.

Al Niyat (sometimes spelled Alniyat) is a name shared by two stars, both of which lie in Scorpio. They act as a "pair" in the imaginary depiction of the scorpion. The name al niyat in Arabic means "the arteries," and if refers to the two stars marking the arteries around the scorpion's heart.

The two Al Niyats in Scorpio.

THE SIGMA SCORPII AL NIYAT.
One of the Al Niyats, also called Sigma Scorpii, is actually a star system rather than a single star. It has a combined magnitude of 2.88 and is located 568 light-years from Earth. The brightest star in the Sigma Scorpii system is a spectroscopic binary star that contains two unresolved stars that orbit each other with a period of approximately 33 days.

THE TAU SCORPII AL NIYAT.
The other Al Niyat is known as Tau Scorpii. Unlike most of the major stars in Scorpio, Tau Scorpii is a single star.
But it is an unusual star.
The Tau Scorpii Al Niyat is a hydrogen fusing dwarf star with a strong and complex magnetic field. An exceptionally hot star, it has a mass 15 times that of the Sun and a radius more than six times that of our Sun. It lies approximately 470 light years from Earth

185

and has an apparent magnitude of 2.8. It is approximately 18,000 times more luminous than our Sun.

The Tau Scorpii Al Niyat is popular with astronomers because it because it has a slow rotation that shows a very clear spectrum and it is quite luminous and hot.

Scorpio contains two meteor showers.

There are two meteor showers associated with Scorpio: the Alpha Scorpiids and the Omega Scorpiids.

ALPHA SCORPIIDS METEOR SHOWER.
The Alpha Scorpiids Meteor shower occurs between April 21 and May 26 every year, with the peak coming about May 15.

They appear only faintly and show up only about three every hour.

Ancients used to think the source of this meteor shower was Antares, but today we know the radiant point is actually from an asteroid located close to Antares classified as Asteroid 2004 BZ74.

THE OMEGA SCORPIIDS METEOR SHOWER.
The Omega Scorpiids Meteor shower actually occurs simultaneously in two slightly

different areas of the sky, both with a radiant point close to the star Omegal Scorpii.

The South Omega Scorpiids meteor shower takes place within the boundaries of constellation of Scorpio. This meteor shower occurs between 23 May- 15 Jun with the peak occurring on the 31-May every year. At its zenith you can typically see five meteors per hour.

The North Omega Scorpiids meteor shower also takes place within the boundaries of the constellation of Scorpio, although in a slightly different part of the sky. It occurs the same dates as the southern shower and the zenith peak also is five per hour.

The Fastest Known Nova is in Scorpio.

A nova is a cataclysmic nuclear explosion in a white dwarf star that occurs as a result of accretion of hydrogen on the star's surface. The accumulated hydrogen ignites, causing nuclear fusion.

One of only ten known reoccurring novas in our Milky Way galaxy, **U Scorpii** is the **fastest known nova**.

Bursts from U Scorpii were observed in 1863, 1906, 1936, 1979, 1987, 1999, and 2010.

U Scorpii normally has a visual magnitude of 18, but during outbursts it reaches magnitude 8. The next burst is expected to occur in the year 2020.

From the dates of observation, the bursts from U Scorpii seem to be increasing in regularity.

Scorpio contains four deep sky or Messier objects.

Messier 4 (M4, NGC 6121), Messier 6 (M6, NGC 6405, often called the "Butterfly Cluster"), Messier 7 (M7, NGC 6475, also referred to as the "Ptolemy Cluster"), and Messier 80 (NGC 6093).

New insights into the meaning of Scorpio?

I t bears pointing out that modern science has shown us that the constellation of Gemini is filled with binary stars and double stars—"twin" stars. And, in a similar way, it has shown us that Scorpio is just as complex as we have always known—because the constellation of Sorpio is filled with complex multiple star systems.

Gemini doubles, Scorpio multiples.

Curious that the ancients knew these things.

It certainly raises the question of how they knew.

We know *Eratosthenes* calculated the circumference of the Earth—correctly—two or three hundred years before the Christian calendar began at 0 A.D. Supposedly with no sort of computer or slide rule or calculator. But really? No advanced mathematical and measurement tools whatsoever? Not even a pencil and paper? Does that not just strain logic just even a little bit? I mean it's not like that's the only thing he worked on his whole life. He wrote a lot, on a lot of different subjects.

If Eratosthenes came up with the circumference of the Earth in his head, without even a pencil and paper, then he must have been some sort of super race with a brain a *whole* lot larger than we have today. Honestly, I still have to struggle to remember the multiplication tables.

Something is missing.

Which brings us to Scorpio. And Dragons.

Dragons are something we think of today as mythological. Our scientists insist they are. At most they are passed off as "simply" ancient artistic descriptions of the most terrifying of ancient predators mashed together into imaginary monsters. They never actually lived on this planet.

And yet, dragons persisted in mythology across the globe in almost every culture. And in cultures that, at least as far as we know, had no connections with each other whatsoever.

And in some of our most ancient past, Scorpio is the astrological sign mostly clearly associated with Dragons. *Nonexistent* Dragons. In the same Scorpio energy we associate with the sign today, **Hidden** Dragons that persist from some ancient, lingering memory but that the (supposedly) rational senses say are not real.

I would suggest this is a deep aspect of Scorpio that we may not give enough credence.

THE

CONSTELLATION OF

OPHIUCHUS

How Ophiuchus was

seen in antiquity.

Ophiuchus was one of the first constellations delineated by Ptolemy in the 2nd Century when he was compiling his great list of 48 Classical Constellations. But there is evidence that the ancient Babylonians knew about the constellation of Ophiuchus, were aware it was located on the ecliptic like the other Zodiac Constellations, but still failed to include it in the Babylonian 12-part division of the astrological Wheel of Life.

Ophiuchus is generally depicted as a man holding a snake. But it is where it is located in the heavens that make it really interesting. Falling smack-dab in the middle of the constellation of Serpens ("the Snake") Ophiuchus imparts something very special to its neighbor, or neighbors depending on how you look at it. Because of Ophiuchus, Serpens is the only constellation in the sky that is divided into two non-contingent parts. Ophiuchus divides the constellation Serpens by severing the snake into two parts: a head and a tail. Ophiuchus is seen as holding the head of the snake with the middle of the snake wrapped around his body and the tail of the snake emerging on the opposite of him.

Long associated with **Asclepius**, the Greek god of Medicine, Ophiuchus is sometimes known by its Latin name Serpentaurius. In English Ophiuchus is usually referred to as "the Snake Bearer" or "the Serpent Charmer."

The star **Serpens Caput** ("the Head of the Snake") literally zigzags vertically along the celestial sphere slightly north of the celestial equator and west of the much larger constellation Ophiuchus—which may be how it got the name since it visually appears to slither like a snake. The star **Serpens Cauda** ("the Tail of the Snake") falls to the east of Ophiuchus.

Asclepius in ancient Greek mythology.

Asclepius was born a demi-god—the son of a mortal woman named **Koronis** and the immortal **Apollo**, the God of Music, Sun and Light, Truth and Prophecy, and Healing. Asclepius's godly heritage was distinctive

194

indeed since **his grandfather was Zeus** himself.

From there, the Greeks have conflicting legends about the life of Asclepius.

One holds that Asclepius's mother Koronis was ashamed that a god had "overtaken" her and that the baby Asclepius was born out of wedlock. So she abandoned baby Asclepius near Epidaurus, leaving him on the ground with a dog and a goat. Protection and milk.

Other legends say that Koronis dared to be unfaithful to Apollo and in a jealous rage Apollo killed her. In those legends, Koronis was pregnant with Asclepius when Apollo killed her and out of guilt, Apollo cut open her stomach and removed her son from her womb before she died—performing **the first birth by Caesarian section**.

But where these two legends meet is that Asclepius, in all the Greek legends, grew up motherless and was reared by his father, the immortal god Apollo. And Apollo gifted his son the **power to heal** and the **secrets of medicine** from plants and herbs just before he turned his son over to Chiron for safekeeping and tutelage.

So, in his youth, Asclepius was **tutored by Chiron**, the oldest and the wisest of the Kentauroi, a race of centaurs who were half-human and half-horse. Chiron, the only

Kentauroi and possibly the only centaur who was immortal, became a centaur by godly magic rather than by birth into the race. He was known as the Greatest of Teachers and The Greatest of Healers.

Chiron taught **Vision and Prophecy as healing arts** and **Healing as Wisdom.**

So from his earliest years, not only was Asclepius partially Divine, but he had the best possible training to heal both with herbs and medicine as well as with prophecy, vision, and wisdom.

Another Greek legend says that the goddess Athena present Asclepius with a vial of magical Gorgon blood. Gorgons were mythical female monster-creatures with huge wings, large bronze claws, snakes growing out of their heads instead of hair, and eyes that could turn a mortal to stone. Gorgon blood was believed to kill a mortal if it was taken from the left side of a Gorgon and to bring a dead mortal back to life if taken from the right side of a Gorgon. Only the greatest of healers had the ability to separate the blood in order to use it wisely.

In the ancient world, snakebite was deadly. For many centuries, even as ancient cultures had developed numerous cures for illnesses, they had no antidotes for snakebite. If you were bitten by a poisonous snake, you died. Period.

WHERE ALPHA MEETS OMEGA

And yet, some early physicians milked snake venom to use it as medicine. How scientific this method was and how often it worked, or even how often the physician lived through his attempt, we are unsure. But there are antiquarian accounts of early attempts to use snake venom as a cure.

We all have seen the depiction of Asclepius. We just didn't know where the depiction came from. Asclepius was always seen in antiquity as a middle-aged man holding a staff with a snake twisted around the staff.

In our modern world, the Rod of Asclepius is the worldwide symbol of Medicine.

Today we call the Rod of Asclepius a **caduceus.**

It is relatively common in the medical community—particularly in the United States—to see a caduceus drawn as a (usually shorter) rod with two winged snakes wrapped around it instead of the longer staff with one snake and no wings.

From the kindest vantage point, this shows a misunderstanding of mythology because that shorter two-snaked symbol actually is the **Wand of Hermes**, a symbol of **commerce**, not a symbol of medicine or healing.

This discrepancy has been pointed out by numerous modern social commentators in recent decades.

And, of course, from the less kind vantage point, as some social commentators such as Stuart L. Tyson have pointed out, this "mistake" may be indicative of the massive problem with modern medicine.

Legends vary about who Asclepius married. But in each, he is credited with fathering many children, all of whom were exceptionally powerful healers.

In some legends, Asclepius married the immortal *Hygeia*, who was also a goddess associated with health—specifically the **Goddess of Good Health** and the **Goddess of Cleanliness and Hygiene**.

Hygeia, by the way, is almost always depicted in classical sculpture as an exceptionally beautiful woman gently holding a snake.

In other legends, Asclepius married the immortal *Epione*, **Goddess of Soothing Pain**.

As many as nine children were supposedly born to Asclepius and his wife. Each was magically powerful as a healer.

Asclepius walked across the world with his magical staff and not only healed many people, but he brought people back from the dead—which sent Hades, the god of the Underworld, into a rage. Hades demanded that Zeus stop Asclepius because the souls of the dead belonged to him. Hades insisted that Asclepius was overstepping his power and had no right to take the dead from him.

Partially concerned with assuaging Hades' anger and partially because Zeus was afraid Asclepius was threatening the balance of nature, Zeus decided he needed to do something. With each "resurrection" to life Asclepius performed, Zeus grew more and more concerned that Asclepius was blurring the lines between mortals and immortals in a way that could not be tolerated. Mortals were supposed to die. Only immortals were supposed to live forever. That was the fundamental Law of Nature.

So unable to reason Asclepius out of his miracles, Zeus struck Asclepius with a lightning bolt and froze him in the sky for the rest of eternity.

Apparently there is life after death, even for a god.

Zeus may have had the power to freeze Asclepius in the sky, but it did not stop humans from seeking miracles. Once seen, a miracle is difficult to put back in the box.

So mortals began erecting temples to Asclepius to be cured of pain and to be healed by Asclepius from heaven.

Often these temples were located near healing waters. And healers gathered at the shrines both to be healed and to learn about the healing arts. Snakes were a big part of the practice at these temples. Non-poisonous snakes roamed freely inside the temples to bring luck, visions of the right healing, and to share with humans their ability to shed their skin in order to be re-born. Since snakes were sacred to Asclepius, snakes were viewed as his conduit from heaven and his gift to mortals.

The specific course of treatment began with the intended patient spending the night in Asclepius' temple, presumably with the snakes. The expectation was that the god himself would appear in a dream to prescribe the exact cure. The next morning the dream would be conveyed to a priest-healer and the right cure would be performed. Right there amid the snakes.

The cult of Asclepius spread all over ancient Greece and the Mediterranean World. Although it declined greatly with the rise of Christianity, ancient sanctuaries dedicated to Asclepius can still be seen today all over Greece. Some of the most famous still-existing temples are at Trikala, Epidaurus, and Kos.

Incidentally, Kos is where the earthly "Father of Medicine" Hippocrates was born and where Hippocrates studied medicine.

What we know about the constellation of Ophiuchus today.

The constellation of Ophiuchus is located northwest of the center of the Milky Way. The northern portion of it divides the constellation of Serpens and is flanked outside of that by the constellations of Aquila and Hercules. The southern portion of Ophiuchus is just east of the constellation of Scorpio and just west of the constellation of Sagittarius.

Ophiuchus is depicted even in the sky as a man holding a snake.
Serpens Caput (the Snake's Head) is on one side of him and *Serpens Cauda* (the Snake's Tail) is on the other. In most

drawings the middle of the snake is somehow wrapped around the man's body.

The star Serpens Caput (the Snake's Head) literally zigzags vertically along the celestial sphere slightly north of the celestial equator and west of the much larger constellation Ophiuchus—which may be how it got the name since it visually appears to slither like a snake. The star Serpens Cauda (the Snake's Tail) falls to the east of Ophiuchus.

Ophiuchus straddles the equator although it lies mostly in the Southern Hemisphere.
During winter in the Northern Hemisphere and during summer in the Southern Hemisphere (November through January primarily), Ophiuchus is in the daytime sky so it is not visible at most latitudes. In the Northern Hemisphere Ophiuchus is finally in the night sky, so it possible to view in the summer.

Notable stars in Ophiuchus.

The brightest star in Ophiuchus is **Rasalhague**, translated from Arabic to mean "head of the serpent charmer." In actuality, Rasalhague (also called Alpha Ophiuchi) is a binary star system with a combined apparent magnitude of 2.08, bright enough to be seen with the naked eye. The primary component of Rasalhague is a white star with a mass about 2.4 times that of our Sun and luminosity 25 times greater than the Sun. Its effective temperature is approximately 8,000 degrees K. And we know it is spinning exceptionally fast. The secondary component of Rasalhague has only about 80 percent the mass of our Sun. And although most of our scientific information on Rasalhague is very new, it appears that the secondary star is a main sequence star still experiencing thermonuclear fusion of hydrogen at its core.

The next brightest star in Ophiuchus is the 2.43 magnitude **Sabik** ("The Preceding One" in Arabic). Sabik is a blue main sequence star that is bright enough to be seen with the naked eye. It is considered the main star in the constellation of Ophiuchus due to its location even though it is not the brightest star in the constellation. The radius of Sabik is 3.30 times that of our Sun. And from our most recent data, Sabik is estimated to be 88.37 light years from Earth.

The third brightest star in the constellation of Ophiuchus is highly unusual **Cebalrai** (the "Dog of the Shepherd"). Cebalrai is a 2.77 apparent magnitude star with about 12.5 times the diameter of our Sun
But Cebalrai is an unusual star for several reasons.

Cebalrai's mass is uncertain at this point although we estimate it is about twice that of our Sun. It appears to be fusing helium into carbon at its deep core, which indicates Cebalrai is an old star that gave up fusion of hydrogen long ago. It is hydrogen fusion that fuels most ordinary stars, our Sun for one.

It is also an oddly variable star, not in brightness but in size. For reasons our scientists don't yet know, Cebalrai seems to jitter or pulse—similar to the pulsation that has been observed in Arcturus. Some astronomers project this jittery quality may mean the star is unstable. But at this point we simply do not know. However, given its apparent age, that could indeed be the case.

Marfik (the Elbow) is a naked-eye star found in Ophiuchus that is actually a binary star with a 3.8 apparent magnitude yellowish white star and a 6.0 magnitude small blue star.

And then, there is **Barnard's Star**, a red-dwarf only about 6 light years away. Well, *only* 6 light years away if light years weren't very far....

Barnard's Star is the fourth closest known star to our Sun. But despite its proximity to us, it is invisible to the naked eye. With an apparent magnitude of a whopping 9.5, it requires significant magnification to see it. Barnard's Star is much brighter in infrared than it is in the visual spectrum.

We know Barnard's Star is a very old star, but despite its age it still experiences star flares, the most recent of which was observed in 1998.

Only named in 2017, Barnard's Star is likely one of the oldest stars in our Milky Way galaxy.

Estimated to be two to three times as old as our Sun, astronomers have argued over the past 60 years whether Barnard's Star had exoplanets orbiting it. The leading proponents projected there was at least one gas giant in orbit around it, but to date no proof of an orbiting gas giant has been found. However, in November 2018, evidence was found of a planet orbiting Barnard's Star that could potentially be a super-Earth. It appears to orbit outside of the star's habitable zone. But some of our most recent information gathered in this area of the galaxy indicates there may be a second orbiting planet we have not yet located.

A particularly intriguing newly found exoplanet.

As recently as December 2009, astronomers determined there may be at least one exoplanet orbiting a star known as Gliese 1214 in Ophiuchus. Further analysis indicates it is the most likely candidate we have found to be an ocean planet. What makes this significant is that the Earth is the only known planet with water on its surface. And humans need liquid water to survive.

Gliese 1214 b is the scientific name for this planet, but astronomers have nicknamed it the "Waterworld."

The Waterworld is only the second super-Earth we have found. A super-Earth is a planet that is larger than the Earth but significantly smaller than our gas giant planets like Saturn and Jupiter in both size and density.

Due to its relative closeness to its sun, the Waterworld seems to have many potential earth-like characteristics. At least compared to most planets we have found thus far.

In December 2013 NASA found what appeared to be clouds in its atmosphere.

The recurrent novae in Ophiuchus.

Believed to be on the brink of becoming a supernova, the recurring nova of RS Ophiuchi falls in the constellation of Ophiuchus. Its brightness is highly variable in irregular intervals that change as much as hundreds of times over a period of a few days.

A rare superbubble in Ophiuchus.

In 2005, astronomers using the world's largest fully steerable radio telescope at the Green Bank Observatory in North Carolina, found evidence of a huge "superbubble" in Ophiuchus.

Scientists are not fully in agreement on precisely what causes a superbubble, but the prevailing thought is that a superbubble is formed by a chain of supernovae, or star explosions. A superbubble is a huge, and by huge I mean hundreds of light years in diameter huge, cavity filled with super-hot gas atoms. Typically a superbubble can be observed only by X-ray emissions from their ultrahot interiors.

But although a superbubble is shaped by a series of destructive forces, they operate much like a gigantic cosmic recycling plant. New stars are formed along the edges of a superbubble where compressed gas leaks through.

The superbubble in Ophiuchus, ever-so-creatively named "The Ophiuchus Superbubble," is large even by superbubble standards. Astronomers tell us that it extends beyond the plane of the galaxy. So any solar births from it may be in our galaxy or in another galaxy.

New insights into the meaning of Ophiuchus.

We may never know why this sign was left out of the astrological Zodiac. And we may not know in our lifetimes if humans ever universally acknowledge Ophiuchus as a sign of the Zodiac.

But here are a few thoughts that may arise in the pondering.

Although the constellation of Ophiuchus falls between our modern constellations of Scorpio and Sagittarius in the sky, when you look at the path of the Sun through Ophiuchus you see an immediate schism between the Sidereal Zodiac and the Tropical Zodiac. Unlike the 12 astrological Zodiac signs, when the Sun is in Ophiuchus, it is **always in Scorpio in the Sidereal Zodiac**. And it is **always in Sagittarius in the Tropical Zodiac**.

The Sun transits through the constellation of Ophiuchus from approximately November 29 to December 17 every year. In the Sidereal Zodiac, that means the Sun is more or less from 12 degrees of Scorpio to the last degree of Scorpio. And in the Tropical Zodiac, the Sun is somewhere between 6 degrees of Sagittarius and 25 degrees of Sagittarius.

Obviously this is partially because the other zodiac signs have been "assigned" equal divisions in the astrological wheel of 30 degrees each and Ophiuchus has no place at the astrological table. The passing of the Sun through Ophiuchus can only be marked visually since it was never allotted space in the astrological Zodiac.

But that Ophiuchus "robs" from Scorpio in the Sidereal Zodiac while it "robs" from Sagittarius in the Tropical Zodiac is an unexpected mathematical anomaly.

But without trying to balance the Sidereal and Tropical Zodiacs, the bridge between Medicine and Belief remains unclear even today.

The "holistic" healing arts of incorporating **wisdom** into both psychological healing and physical healing seem to be sought after but still just outside the grasp of humanity.

The balancing of Vision and Prophecy and "faith healing" with hard-core scientific medicine is a fragile one for many people. The question of heavenly intervention and heavenly "magical" cure is one mankind still grapples with today. And the question of just how aggressively mortal life can be, and should be, extended by medicine remain unanswered. As a society even if not as an individual.

And in a world where modern medicine routinely sends huge bolts of electricity through a human body when it stops breathing or the heart stops beating to bring the patient "back to life," it seems oddly like what Zeus was trying to prevent. And yet, eerily like what Zeus did to Asclepius to end Asclepius's life on Earth.

The kidneys stop functioning. Our medicine steps in an extends life by sticking large needles into the veins, forcing the blood out of the body, filtering the blood, then forcing it back into to the body—to keep the person alive.

A human dying of cancer is stuck with large needles and pumped full of enough poison to kill his cells just short of killing the person—in order to keep him alive. Of course, we call it chemotherapy, not snake venom. A patient in a coma unable to breathe or eat or drink is needled and tubed to force him to breathe and to accept nutrition and hydration. Without the person's permission and very often against the person's will.

These are common medical procedures in our modern world and our very advanced state of modern medicine.

But one wonders in reading the ancient myths associated with the constellation of Ophiuchus if that might not have been the whole point of Zeus's concern. And why Zeus blasted Asclepius into the sky to create Ophiuchus in the first place.

The needles and tubes in modern hospitals may be more like the snakes in those old Greek temples than we realize.

Boundaries between Life and Death. Or Lifetime and Lifetime. Those boundaries are imponderable for most of us and filled with mysticism for many. And clearly, since time immemorial the questions of what is natural and what is unnatural about human mortality have plagued man.

And maybe even God.

And apparently, it is a riddle even Zeus could not solve.

Even if Ophiuchus is never a sign in the astrological Zodiac, it provides food for thought—lodged right there between the astrological sign of Life and Death (Scorpio) and the astrological sign of Philosophy and Religion (Sagittarius).

And yet, we know the Zodiac has changed before.

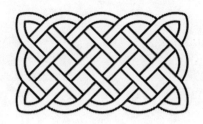

THE

CONSTELLATION OF

SAGITTARIUS

How Sagittarius was

seen in antiquity.

Sagittarius is one of the 48 constellations listed by the 2nd century astronomer Ptolemy and remains one of the 88 modern constellations.

Ancient Babylonians identified Sagittarius as the God *Nergal*, a strange centaur-like creature firing an arrow from a bow. He is generally depicted with the body of a horse with wings and two heads. One head was a panther head, and the other head was a human head. And above the conventional horse's tail was a stinger resembling a scorpion's tail.

The Sumerian name for Sagittarius was *Pabuksag*. The name came from two Sumerian words: *Pabil*, meaning "older paternal kinsman," and *Sag*, meaning "chief or head." Roughly translated this would mean **forefather** or **chief ancestor**.

Although neither the Babylonian or the Sumerian symbols match our modern concept of Sagittarius, they clearly form the historical and mythological basis for it. And over time, the concept seemed to continually morph.

In Greek mythology Sagittarius is identified as a Centaur: half human, half horse. At least that is what some modern writers say.

But in Greek legend, there are actually **two Centaurs associated with constellations** and at least a dozen conflicting myths about them.

The **Centaur named Sagittarius** is one, but probably the more significant Centaur was the **Centaur named Chiron**, known as the Wisest and Most Just of the Centaurs. The two are often mistakenly interchangeably referred to as "the centaur," but their mythologies are very different. And, in fact, Chiron resides in a whole different constellation of the sky called Centaurus.

But some Greek legends say the Centaur in Sagittarius was not a Centaur at all, but rather a Satyr.

In Greek mythology, a Satyr was a type of lustful, drunken woodland or mountain god that was often depicted as a man with a horse's ears and tail and a permanent over-exaggerated erection.

About two centuries B.C., the great Greek mathematician and astronomer Eratosthenes wrote that the figure in Sagittarius was actually the **Satyr named Crotus**. By the time Eratosthenes lived, Satyrs were often drawn as having human legs rather than horse legs, although the close connection to a horse remained. Satyrs evolved from having horse legs to almost always being seen on horseback.

The Greek legends Eratosthenes retold held that the Satyr *Crotus* was the **inventor of the hunting bow**, of **archery**, and of the **rhythmic beats used to accompany music**. But even more than he loved playing music, Crotus loved hunting in the wilderness. He was considered to be **the most skillful of shooters**. And he dearly **loved music**. According to the writings of Eratosthenes, Crotus lived most of his life among the Muses and it was the Muses who were responsible for his eternal resting place with his bow and arrow on his horse (or on his horse legs) in the sky.

I will add a side note here that Eratosthenes was the chief librarian of the Great Library of Alexandria and an unbelievably well-educated scholar.

Eratosthenes calculated the circumference of the Earth about 200 years before the birth of Jesus in Bethlehem. And his calculation was an exact measurement within two percent of the circumference of the Earth NASA uses today. So this guy was no dumb caveman. If he says Sagittarius was originally a Satyr and not a Centaur, I personally am inclined to believe him.

Whatever or whoever holds it, the arrow of this constellation points directly towards the star Antares, the "heart of the scorpion."

Some legends say Sagittarius is positioned in the sky ever ready to avenge Scorpius's slaying of Orion. Other legends say he is poised to defend Hercules if Hercules is ever attacked by Scorpius. But regardless of the version of legend, the "enemy" is the Scorpion and the tip of the arrow in Sagittarius' bow is aimed for the heart.
Mistrustful of his neighbor for sure.

The description of Sagittarius in *Astrologia Restaurata* by William Ramesey in 1653 in London:

> **The ninth sign is called
> Sagittarius (signifying an
> Archer or one using to cast
> darts) because the Sun being
> therein, the heat is overcome by**

218

cold, whereupon ensue Fogs and Frosts, and such like, being (for the nature of the mischief and hurt they do) as obnoxious, or equivalent to venomous Arrows or Darts.

Apparently, Ramesey also really disliked winter. But then he lived in London, right?

What we know about the constellation of Sagittarius today.

First recorded by the Greek astronomer Ptolemy in the 2nd Century, the constellation of Sagittarius is the largest constellation in the southern hemisphere and the 15th largest constellation in the sky. It occupies 867 square degrees and is clearly visible to the naked eye.

Sagittarius sits at the center of our Milky Way galaxy where the galaxy is its most dense. Because of this, Sagittarius is often associated with the Galactic Center.

The constellation of Sagittarius borders Capricornus and Scorpius, but also the constellations of Aquila, Scutum, Cauda,

Ophiuchus, Corona, Australis, Telescopium, Indus, and Microscopium.

Sagittarius is visible between 55 degrees and -90 degrees in the sky, and is best viewed in the Northern Hemisphere during the month of August around 9 PM.

It is a bright constellation situated in a densely-filled area of the sky with many bright stars. In fact, **seven of the stars in Sagittarius are brighter than the 3rd magnitude**. And part of Sagittarius is relatively close to the Earth with three of its stars less than 33 light-years away.

In addition, we know today that Sagittarius is filled with planets. At least 32 of the stars in Sagittarius are circled by known planets.

This constellation has been "seen" as different things by different peoples. One envisioning of Sagittarius is as the "Milk Dipper," a plain outline that looks much like the Little Dipper, only smaller.

Others saw it as a giant "Teapot." And, in fact, most drawings of the constellation in star maps strongly resemble such a teapot.

To see the stars aligned as a Centaur or an archer takes a great deal more imagination and latitude. But within the outline of three of the brightest stars, a bow can be seen without much stretch of imagination. Those three stars, all with Arabic names, mark the northern, middle, and southern parts of the bow.

Kaus Borealis ("the northern bow" or the "north part of the bow" in Arabic) marks the top of the bow.

Kaus Media, marks the middle of the bow.

And **Kaus Australis**, the southernmost part of it.

Then to "tip" it off, is the star **Al Nasl** (sometimes Alnasl), which in Arabic means "the arrowhead," positioned just where the tip of the arrow would lie in the bow. *Al Nasl* actually almost glitters at times since it is in actually a double star with the main star a 3rd magnitude star that has a 4.7 apparent magnitude companion that is a Cepheid variable.

These four stars, Kaus Borealis, Kaus Media, Kaus Australis, and Al Nasl, are part of a group of eight extremely bright stars in Sagittarius that form an asterism, or star pattern. We typically call this eight-star asterism the archer's bow and arrow. That's where the Centaur or Archer comes from.

The tip of the arrow is pointed directly at the heart of the Scorpion.

Several of the stars in this constellation are extremely large, some as much is 11 times the size of our solar system's Sun.

Sagittarius is situated in such a dense section of the Milky Way that even some extremely bright stars found in it are difficult to see with the naked eye.

A good example of this is the **Pistol Star**, a bright blue hyper giant that is one of the brightest stars ever discovered. But despite its brightness, it is barely visible to the naked eye because there is so much interstellar dust around it. The Pistol Star was not found until 1990 when it was discovered by an astronomer at UCLA using the Hubble telescope. It may be what scientists call a luminous blue variable star, but that determination is yet to be made. We do know, however, it is one of the most luminous stars known. The Pistol Star has a luminosity 1,600,000 times that of our Sun. It is simply in such a dense and bright section of the sky, in the middle of the Milky Way, that it took deep magnification to find it.

The Pistol Star is part of an area full of massive young stars called the Quintuplet Cluster near the center of our galaxy.

The Black Hole at the center of our universe is in Sagittarius.

Within this same area of space is a bright radio source known as Sagittarius A* (pronounced Sagittarius A-star). This bright radio source is actually is a **black hole right in the center of the galaxy**.

Sagittarius A* is the nearest black hole to Earth. Because of its proximity to us, Sagittarius A* is the epicenter of modern black hole research.

You might recall that in the beginning of this book I mentioned that our scientific information is growing unbelievably rapidly, that new discoveries about our universe are being made monthly if not weekly.

Well, I would be remiss to not share a very new finding right here—oddly enough right here next to the black hole.

This book was originally set to be released on **April 14 of 2019**. The following paragraph was written as the last sentence in this section on the black hole in Sagittarius:

"At this point in our technology, we cannot see a black hole directly, but we can observe how it affects the stars around it, which is how black holes are located."

But on **April 3, 2019**—eleven days before this book was set for launch—the National Science Foundation in the United States released a photograph of a black hole!

The first-ever photograph of a black hole is evidence of the first direct visual observation of a black hole, ever. The black hole photographed was not in this sector of Sagittarius, but in Virgo.

I simply could have corrected the sentence from several weeks ago. But the full information underscores how truly rapidly Earth's space exploration is expanding our knowledge about the physical universe.

Nebulae & Galaxies in Sagittarius.

The same region also contains several nebulae. One is called the **Lagoon Nebula**, a massive interstellar cloud approximately 50 light-years by 110 light-years in diameter.

And two others, the **Omega Nebula** and the **Trifid Nebula**, also appear in Sagittarius. Both the Omega Nebula and the Trifid Nebula are considered star nurseries because they appear to constantly be birthing dozens of new stars.

And it is in this area of Sagittarius that the **Dwarf Elliptical Galaxy** was found, the first globular cluster ever discovered outside of the Milky Way.

New insights into the meaning of Sagittarius?

I am going to circle back to the timing of the first ever photograph of a black hole that was released within a matter of days of the release of this book.

The director of the scientific group who took the photograph of the first-ever-seen black hole said in a public statement along with a release of the photograph:

"We have seen what we thought was the unseeable."

Although that photograph was taken of a black hole in the constellation of Virgo, not in Sagittarius, the "unseeable" which is now *seen* resonates for all black holes. And remember, we have a great big black hole right in the middle of Sagittarius, which sits right at the middle of our galaxy.

Our science is changing our very "sight." And the change is happening far more rapidly than most of us realize.

And, if symbolism of the skies, as the ancients believed, is true, this seeing of the unseeable may be a harbinger of major breakthroughs for humans in other ways too. In ways we cannot *foresee*.

It is likely no accident that the same constellation of Sagittarius is filled with lots and lots of very bright stars in such close proximity to a vast black hole very near to the center of our galaxy. In fact, the contrast is so stark and the stars in that area so bright that one of the brightest stars is in Sagittarius was almost too bright for us to see.

The sheer brilliance of the Pistol Star in Sagittarius is almost beyond the ability of most of use to fully comprehend. More than one-and-a-half MILLION times brighter than our Sun!

Whether there is a repeatable physical relation to proximity of a black hole and the ultra brightness of the stars close to it, we do not yet know scientifically. But we very well may soon know.

And then there is the lost symbolism of the Satyr.

Not only has modern astrology at least partially lost the Centaur symbolism to replace it with a far more simplistic concept of an archer, but it turns out the ancients might actually have viewed Sagittarius more as a Satyr than as a Centaur anyway.

That's certainly what the guy who measured the girth of the Earth in his head said.

Brand new pictures for the brain. Well, brand   new   ancient   pictures.

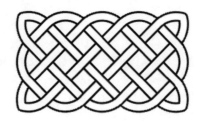

THE

CONSTELLATION OF

CAPRICORN

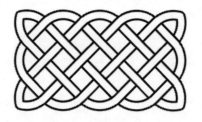

How Capricorn was

seen in antiquity.

The sign of Capricornus (or what we today call Capricorn) is represented by the "horned goat" or as "having horns like a goat."

But in antiquity Capricornus was represented by a type of Centaur—a Sea-Goat—a mythological being that is half goat and half fish.

Capricorn is the smallest of the Zodiac Constellations, yet it has one of the oldest mythological associations of the zodiac.

In the oldest accounts, the date the Sun entered into Capricorn marked the Winter Solstice.

The Sea-Goat mythology of Capricorn dates back more than 3,000 years.

The constellation we now call Capricorn was explicitly recorded in the Babylonian star catalogs as the "Goat Fish" some time before 1000 BC.

The Sea-Goat persisted through most of Greek mythology.

According to ancient Greek myths, the constellation of Capricorn started with the Sea-Goat **Pricus**, who was the father of race of Centaurs called Sea-Goats. These creatures, half goat and half fish, were intelligent and honorable citizens. They lived in the sea near the shore. They could think and they could even speak, according to the Greek legends. And they were such a noble race that they were greatly favored by the gods.

Pricus, the father of this great race, shared Kronos' ability to **manipulate time** and he also was apparently very busy because legend says *Pricus* had lots and lots of children who all lived near the seashore and who loved to play on the beach. His Sea-Goat children kept climbing out of the sea to go onto dry land.

According to the legends, when Pricus' little Sea-Goats found themselves on the dry land, they turned into normal goats and lost

231

their special ability to think and to speak in the process. They became dumb goats. And this grieved Pricus greatly.

So, partially to prevent the dumbing of his little Sea-Goat children and partially to keep them from continually leaving him, Pricus turned back time again and again.

But still his children clamored for the land. The sea was not enough to keep them happy.

So Pricus eventually resigned himself to loneliness and misery and let the little Sea-Goats leave. Learning he could not control the fate of his children, but not wanting to be the only Sea-Goat left, Pricus begged Kronos to let him die.

Kronos understood Pricus's plight with his children, but Pricus was immortal so Kronos could not allow him to die. The compromise was that Kronos allowed Pricus to spend eternity in the sky as Capricorn—so he could at least eternally watch over his little ones, dumb as they might be.

Who says the Greeks didn't have a sense of humor?

In Cretan mythology, the constellation we call Capricorn was sometimes connect with Amalthea, the goat that suckled the infant Zeus after his mother, Rhea, saved him from being devoured by his father, Kronos (or Chronos).

232

Although there are multiple versions of mythology about Amalthea, in at least some of them, her broken horn was transformed into the **Horn of Plenty**, or the **cornucopia**.

Most of the Cretan legends about Amalthea seem to indicate she was no longer a Sea-Goat, but was one of the descendants of Pricus who had become a land goat.

The Sea-Goat was lost by modern times.

Ramesey's 1653 description of Capricorn was:

> *The tenth sign is named Capricornius (signifying a Goat) because the Sun being therein is farthest from the vertical point; so that by reason of the cold mixed with dryness, and the want of heat, which at that to time is, the nature and disposition of the ayr is melancholy, after the nature of the Goat.*

By the 17th Century, the concept of a Sea-Goat or any kind of connection to water with Capricorn seems to be altogether gone.

What we know about the constellation of Capricorn today.

The constellation of Capricorn is located in an area of sky called the **Sea**. It sits among other constellations of the water genre including the Water Bearer Aquarius, the Sea Monster Cetus, the Fishes of Pisces, and the River of Eridanus.

The constellation of Capricornus, what we today call Capricorn, is among the faintest constellations in the sky. It is slightly brighter than the constellation of Cancer. Capricorn measures 414 square degrees, making it the 40th largest constellation. It is the smallest of the Zodiac Constellations.

Capricorn is visible between latitudes 60 degrees and -90 degrees and is best viewed during the month of September around 9 PM.

The constellation of Capricorn in the sky appears as a slightly deformed triangle with the longest line on the top and the "tip" of the triangle pointing downward. Some describe it as an arrowhead shape.

To find it Capricorn in the sky, look for the summer triangle and make a line from the star *Vega* through the star *Altair* to the lower southern sky.

The Tropic of Capricorn is the place where the sun appears overhead at noon on the winter solstice. It was originally sliced right through its namesake constellation, however the line has since shifted into the constellation of Sagittarius due to precession of the equinoxes.

The brightest stars in Capricorn.

The brightest star in the constellation of Capricorn is **Deneb Algedi** (also called Delta Capricorni), at a magnitude of 2.85.

The Arabic word deneb means tail.

Deneb Algedi is in actuality not just one star, but part of a four-star system that can be seen with the naked eye. Astronomers are not sure exactly how to classify Deneb Algedi except that it is among the brightest of the "metallic A stars," extremely hot stars that are highly enriched in most metals but with significant deficiencies in other elements such as calcium.

The second brightest star in Capricorn is **Dabih** (Beta Capricorni). Dabih is also a multiple-star system, but a highly complex system.

In fact, Dabih is such a huge and complex multiple-star system that, as the modern professor emeritus of astronomy at the University of Illinois Jim Kahler says, Dabih alone could be an astronomer's lifetime study.

Among the eccentricities of Dabih, two of the many pairs of stars within it are at least 21,000 times as far apart from each other as the earth is from our Sun.

In what is called the "belly of the goat," there is a star named **Omega Capricorni** that is a red giant with highly variable luminosity and magnitude. Astronomers are uncertain exactly how to classify it and currently give it both a K and an M giant designation. Its variability and temperature remain unmeasured. Curiously, Omega Capricorni did not seem to be a star important enough to the ancient Arabic astrologers to even name.

Unusual deep space objects found in Capricorn.

A globular star cluster named **Messier 30** is in the southern part of the constellation of Capricorn near the barium star zZeta Capricorni.

M30, as it is referred to, was part of the original discovery of Charles Messier, the 18th Century French astronomer.

Scientists tell us that the M30 cluster has already passed through a dynamic process called a core collapse. And as a result it now has a core mass approximately one million times that of our Sun. We know that stars that dense in proximity experience a high rate of interactions that birth binary star systems. And often mass transfer in these areas also create the type of star we call a Blue Straggler.

It is estimated that the M30 star cluster is about 12.93 billion years old and it has a combined mass about 160,000 times that of our Sun.

M30 appears to have a retrograde orbit that suggests to our scientists that it came from a satellite galaxy rather than having its birth inside our Milky Way Galaxy.

New insights into the meaning of Capricorn?

A student of mine who was a serious student of ancient mythology once remarked that the myth of Pricus and how he came to be in the sky as the constellation Capricorn seemed eerily like the story of Evolution—just backwards. Instead of growing smarter and wiser, the little Sea-Goats grew dumber.

Except maybe the story was not intended to be a story about Evolution at all. But about Devolution.

Our science doesn't really delve into Devolution. But if you think about it, that same theme of Devolution may underlie part of the Libra mythology as well—when mankind became so vile and base that Astraea chose to simply leave Earth.

We do see, however, a glimmer of our current understanding of Capricorn in the old myths about the Sea-Goats. Today we see the Capricorn goat as a climber, one who can climb to the top of the mountain peak against all odds. That part of our concept seems to be an echo of the Sea-Goats climbing all the way out of the sea to become land animals. From mystical to real.

But also from immortal to mortal.

Again, it seems like a story of Devolution rather than of Evolution, doesn't it?

But then, maybe Evolution and Devolution are a lot like East and West or Up and Down. It may all depend on what direction you view it from.

From our new science.

Two things stand out about Capricorn from our newest scientific information.

One is that the three brightest stars in the constellation of Capricorn defy all classifications our science has for stars.

And the second one, a fact that may be integrally tied to the first, is that the deep sky of Capricorn holds a massive star cluster filled with star clusters that originate from a whole other galaxy.

The coming conjunction of Saturn and Pluto in Capricorn.

In less than a year from the date this book was written, the planets of Saturn and Pluto will exact a conjunction in the sign of Capricorn. This will be the first time these two planets have been in exact conjunction in the sign of Capricorn in 502 years.

Last time it happened, it took Christianity from a "one church" structure centered in Rome to a wide splay of fledgling Protestant sects all over the world. The Great Sea-Goat had to watch all the little Sea-Goats leave the "one Sea" and clamor towards land. It did seem to have a splintering effect that is not fully described by the modern concept of Capricorn. And yet, it oddly fits with the ancient a lot more.

What will this coming major conjunction hold? We don't fully know. But it may far more reflect the ancient concept of the Sea-Goat than the modern Mountain Goat.

THE

CONSTELLATION OF

AQUARIUS

How Aquarius was seen in antiquity.

Aquarius is one of the oldest recognized constellations in the zodiac and was one of the 48 constellations listed by the second century astronomer Ptolemy. It remains one of the 88 modern constellations.

Aquarius is found in the region of the sky often called the Sea—along with a profusion of constellations with watery associations such as Cetus the Whale, Pisces the Fish, and Eridanus the River.

This may be why many modern people think of Aquarius as a water sign even though in our modern zodiac it is designated an air sign.

But certainly in ancient mythology, Aquarius is all about water.

In Sumerian mythology, the youth known as **Aquarius** brought a destructive flood that ravaged the entire planet.

Some antiquarians see this Sumerian legend as the same story that was written about as the Great Flood in the Old Testament of the Bible associated with Noah and his Ark.

The Sumerian version says that Aquarius held the vessel from which the floodwaters flowed from the heavens onto the earth. Aquarius is depicted as the **facilitator of the flood**.

Pretty much a bad guy—unless you believe all the creatures on Earth really needed dying.

Modern archaeologists have found ancient Babylonian star figures on stones and cylinder seals from the 2nd millennium. In earliest known Babylonian astronomical records, Ea was the ruler of the southernmost quarter of the sun's path, called the "Way of Ea."

Aquarius was specifically associated with the cyclical destructive floods that the Babylonians experienced in the summer. When the month of rain came, Babylonians called it the "curse of rain." To the Babylonians, Aquarius was not exactly loved.

In ancient Egyptian astronomy, Aquarius also was associated with flooding. But in Egypt, the dreaded flooding was the annual flood of the Nile. The Nile's banks were said to flood when Aquarius put his jar into the river at the beginning of each spring

The constellation of Aquarius was called a name meaning the "Water Pitcher" in the Hindu zodiac as well.

Other Greek and Roman mythologies about the constellation of Aquarius.

Sometimes in Greek mythology Aquarius is seen as **the son of Prometheus**, who built a ship with his wife to survive an eminent flood. This myth seems to clearly mirror the story of Noah and the Ark in the Bible.

But in some Greek myths, Aquarius is identified as the beautiful youth *Ganymede* who was **the son of the Trojan King Tros** who was taken to Mount Olympus by Zeus to act as a Cup Carrier to the gods.
Several versions of Ganymede's adventures run through Greek mythology.
In some versions, Zeus sent his pet **Eagle Aquila** to snatch Ganymede. In other versions of the myth **Zeus disguised himself as an eagle** and stole Ganymede in order to make him a cup carrier to the gods. And in still other versions, it was the Goddess of the Dawn **Eos**, motivated by her affection for beautiful young men, who stole

Ganymede—and then Zeus stole Ganymede from Eos and eventually employed him as Cup Bearer.

The Roman version of the myth is very similar to the Greek. But the Roman names for the gods are different. Zeus is Jupiter. Aquarius is sometimes called **Ganymedes** and sometimes called **Catamitus**, the beautiful son of the King of Troy.

Although the earliest forms of the myth of Ganymede from the Greeks, and even the earliest Roman forms, have no erotic content, by the 5th Century B.C., it changed. The later stories of Ganymede (Ganymedes or Catamitus) seem to have an overlay of a kidnapper god who had a homosexual passion for the youth. The kidnapping of Ganymede appears frequently as artwork on 5th Century Attic vases.

The concept of the constellation of Aquarius in other parts of the ancient world.

In Arab mythology, Aquarius is neither a being nor God.
He's a bucket.
Most scholars believe this version is directly linked to the Arab religious belief that forbids any kind of depictions of living

forms or beings. But clearly the vessel holding or carrying water remains the theme.

No matter which myth one may follow, the basic concept of Aquarius is pretty much the same.

Aquarius has never, even in the most remote antiquity, been viewed as a creature of the water. It is instead a facilitator of water, a manipulator of water. And, almost always, was directed by a higher power. Or at least by a power that was beyond the control of man.

In the 17th century A.D., according to William Ramesey in his *Astrologia Restaurata*, the nature of Aquarius was seen as:

> *The eleventh sign is called Aquarius (signifying a Waterman, or one pouring water) because when the Sun is in this sign, dryness is overcome by moisture beginning, yet the cold remaining which causeth the temper of the ayr to be cold and moist, after the nature of water.*

So by the 17th Century A.D., we begin to clearly see the explicit concept of dryness and air   associated   with   Aquarius.

What we know about the constellation of Aquarius today.

The constellation of Aquarius is a large but faint constellation in the southern sky.

Aquarius is one of the oldest documented constellations, recorded by the Sumerians many centuries before it was listed as a constellation by the Greek astronomer Ptolemy in the 2nd Century A.D.

It is located near the other water-related constellations: Cetus the Whale, Pisces the Fishes, Delphinus the Dolphin, and Eridanus the River in the section of the sky often called the Sea.

Aquarius is the 10th largest constellation in the sky and is spread out over 980 square degrees.

There are, however, no particularly bright stars in the constellation so it can be difficult to see with the naked eye.

Aquarius is visible between 65 degrees and -90 degrees and can be seen in the spring in the Southern Hemisphere, and the fall in the Northern Hemisphere. It is best viewed during the month of October around 9 PM in the Northern Hemisphere. But you often need some sort of magnification even in peak season.

The brightest stars in Aquarius.

The brightest star in Aquarius is a rare yellow supergiant known as **Sadlsuud** (or Beta Aquarii). *Sadlsuud* is 600 light-years from Earth and has a magnitude of 2.9, which is very low.

Sadalmelik (Alpha Aquarii) is a giant star located in Aquarius that is 760 light-years from Earth with the magnitude of 2.95.

Sadachbia (Gamma Aquarii) which is 158 light-years from Earth with the magnitude of 3.8 is also in Aquarius.

Zeta Aquarii, which sits at the center of the Y-shaped configuration that forms

Aquarius' water jar, curiously has no given name other than its brightness classification of "zeta."

Aquarius and the star Fomalhaut.

The stream of water coming out of the jar is made up of more than 20 stars ending with the star **Fomalhaut**, that today falls in the neighboring constellation of Piscis Austrinus.

You may remember that in Ptolemy's 2nd Century star catalog that Formalhaut was one of the stars he listed twice—once as being in the constellation of Aquarius and once as being in the constellation of Piscis Austrinus.

Today, Fomalhaut is considered solely in the constellation of Piscis Austrinus even though the flow of water from the jar of Aquarius ends there.

Other interesting "occupants" of the constellation of Aquarius.

The constellation of Aquarius also includes a number of planetary nebulae, including one of the brightest nebulae in the sky, NGC 7009. Also known as the **Saturn Nebula** because of the ring it has resembling Saturn, NGC 7009 was first observed in 1782 by Sir William Herschel, the German-born British astronomer who is credited with discovery of the planet Uranus.

The closest of all planetary nebulae to our Earth is NGC 7293, often called the **Helix Nebula**, is also found in the Aquarius constellation.

Potential homes for man in Aquarius.

In 2017, astronomers found the ultracool star TRAPPIST-1 in the constellation of Aquarius. TRAPPIST-1 is only 40 light-years from Earth and about ten times the distance from Earth to the nearest star system of Alpha Centauri.

TRAPPIST-1 hosts at least seven exoplanets.

All seven of these exoplanets are Earth-sized worlds and are likely also rocky. Many of these planets orbit in the habitable region of the star, defined as the zone in which water could exist on the planets' surfaces, depending on specifics of each planet's atmosphere.

Astronomers note that all seven worlds circling TRAPPIST-1 orbit closer to their sun than the planet Mercury orbits the Sun in our own solar system. But since the sun in their system is an ultracool star, the environments of these planets are not nearly as hot as they would be in our solar system at the same proximity from the sun.

We will have a better look at these planets when NASA's James Webb Space Telescope (the "next generation" of the Hubble telescope) launches in March of 2021.

Astronomers are eagerly awaiting study of TRAPPIST-1 in an ongoing effort to better understand universal characteristics of earth-sized, rocky planets similar to our Earth.

New insights into the meaning of Aquarius.

I have to admit that in reading the ancient mythology about the sign of Aquarius it is clear the concept of the sign has changed, significantly. And yet, I have a difficult time gaining serious insight into the sign from the ancient myths. Strain as I might, they simply seem oddly disconnected from everything I have studied or observed about the sign of Aquarius over the course of my lifetime.

In fact, I even wonder if the constellation is the same constellation.

Though clearly part of ancient flood stories and clearly conveying how fearful ancient people were of floods, it is difficult to grasp much meaningful insight from the ancient myths.

Perhaps in reading the old stories they will bring more insight to you than to me. I hope so.

From our latest science, however, it appears the Aquarius constellation may soon clarify some Laws of the Universe.

Our understanding of that sector of the sky is very recent. But it appears to be growing extremely rapidly.

The 2021 premiere of the James Webb telescope is certainly poised to examine life and the sustaining atmospheres for life in ways that may change us forever.

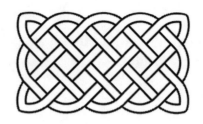

THE

CONSTELLATION OF

PISCES

How Pisces was seen in

antiquity.

Oddly, it is the myths that lead up to Pisces that are the most indicative of the constellation of Pisces.
So let's start pre-Pisces just a tiny bit.

The wandering eye of Zeus and the wrath of Hera.

In Greek legend the King of the Gods Zeus and his wife Hera had a troubled marriage, to say the least.

A great number of Greek legends grow out of this tragic pairing of two immortals bound together in wedlock—forever—who seem to hate each other as much as they love each other.

Zeus had a horribly wandering eye for other women. And, as the most powerful of the gods, Zeus was able to use elaborate magical trickery to seduce women. One thing you can say about Zeus is that he was an equal opportunity seducer. Immortal or mortal. Mount Olympus or a remote field of flowers on the Earth. He seduced women. And being the great He-God that he was, a baby was almost always a result of one of his trysts.

Not too surprisingly, these dalliances did not go over well with Zeus's wife Hera. She often was filled with rage. And insanely jealous. And since Hera was both immortal and magically powerful, being the object of Hera's wrath was dangerous and seldom ended well.

So, after one of Zeus's many seductions beyond the marital bed, Hera enticed the Earth goddess Gaia to fall in love with the horrible Tartarus who was called by the ancient Greeks "the Bottomless Pit." Since it was a magical love affair, Gaia and Tartarus had a horrible offspring—intentionally engineered by Hera to be an unbeatable foe of Zeus's. The child of that awful union was named **Typhoeus**.

Yes, the root of the word "typhoid," as in the killer disease typhoid fever.

Legend says that Typhoeus was a monstrous giant who was so tall his head touched the stars. His torso was that of a man but his legs were coils of vipers that could strike as Typhoeus walked. Since he had several heads, he could strike numerous people at once simply by walking past them.

According to the legend, Typhoeus' main head had one hundred vipers growing out of it that made the sounds of one hundred different animals. Typhoeus had a filthy, matted beard, pointed ears, and eyes that glowed red, He breathed fire, he had hundreds of wings sprouted from his body, and from each hand grew one hundred dragon's heads.

Needless to say, Typhoeus was the most powerful and the most fearful god of Greek legend. He was a monster.

But he was also a god.

Not a good combination.

And all as a result of Hera's righteous anger towards her husband.

So one day, when Typhoeus was finally fully grown, Hera ordered him to kill Zeus and the gods that she considered the cause of Zeus' infidelities—like the goddess of Beauty, **Aphrodite**, and the god of Sexual Love, **Eros**. You may know these two gods from their later Roman renaming as Venus and Cupid.

Being the kind of horrible creature he was, Typhoeus gladly followed Hera's command

and what ensured was a war that lasted, according to legend, ten thousand years.

Greek legend is filled with encounters where Typhoeus destroyed whole cities and yanked mountains out of the ground to throw them into the sky. In fact, in one battle he almost killed the immortal Zeus.

Almost.

Then one day, when Typhoeus was particularly angry, he shouted out that he was going to end Zeus and all the gods *that* day.

And as Typoeus began marching towards Mount Olympus, all of the gods began turning themselves into unrecognizable animals in hopes of escaping the edges of his wrath.

Aphrodite, the goddess of Beauty, and her son **Eros** the god of Sexual Love, were standing near a peaceful pond so they decided turn themselves into **two koi fish**. But the pond was filled with koi fish and they wanted to **stay together** and **feared getting lost among the other fish**, so they **bound their tails together**. But they were almost too late because Typhoeus saw them jump into the water and he reached into the water to grab them. Not knowing the pond, they didn't know how to find safety, but other fish took **mercy** on them showed them how to **dive to the bottom of the pond** to be **hidden**. And so they escaped.

And they lived to keep **Beauty** and **Sexual Love** alive in the world.

So, as the legend goes, to commemorate how important the survival of Beauty and Sexual Love was for the world, Zeus placed Aphrodite and Eros, along with the kind fish who saved them, in the sky for eternity as the constellation of Pisces.

This legend is one of many Greek legends that the Romans took whole and simply re-named the characters by Roman names. In Roman mythology, this is the myth not of Typhoeus, Aphrodite and Eros, but of *Typhon*, *Venus* and *Cupid*. But it is the same myth. At least sometimes.

As with many legends, there is a variation on the story associated with the constellation of Pisces. It starts the same, but there is a twist. Whether the variation was Greek, whether it preceded the other legend or followed the other legend, or whether the Romans simply changed the Greek legend, we don't know.

But the other account comes from the great Roman poet Ovid (1 B.C.-1 A.D.).

It goes like this.

Aphrodite (Dione in the original text, also called Venus by the Romans) and her small son Eros (Cupidos in the Roman text, also Cupid) were running from Mount

Olympus to escape Typhoeus (Typhon). Aphrodite, with tiny Cupidos in tow, ran all the way to the Euphrates River. It being too wide to cross, she hid them both in the tall reeds among a grove of poplars and willows at the edge of the river bank, hoping Typhoeus would not see them there. But when Aphrodite heard the roaring Typhoeus approach, she became very afraid he would find them, so she clutched her child to her breast and prayed "To the rescue, Nymphae (Nymphs), and bring help to two divinities." At that she leap into the river clutching Eros tightly. Immediately, large Syrian river fish (the Ichthyes) swam beneath their feet and carried them to safety.

According to this version of the legend, and echoed even today in parts of the Middle East, the Syrians refuse to eat fish in gratitude to the Ichthyes.

And, interestingly, some antiquarians say the two fish who saved Aphrodite and Eros in this legend were probably the same, or possibly slightly re-imagined, as the Ichthyocentaurs (or Fish-Centaurs) named **Aphros** and **Bythos** who were widely depicted in late classical art bringing Aphrodite ashore after her birth. That legend, of course, is tied to the ancient legend associated with the constellation of Cancer.

But, as most legends, part of it was lost over time. By the 17th Century, Pisces was looked upon much more clinically.

British astrologer William Ramesey wrote
of Pisces in 1653:

> *The twelfth sign is named Pisces*
> *(signifying Fishes) for that when*
> *the Sun is therein, the ayr it is*
> *inclined to cold and moisture,*
> *yet having some small heat,*
> *after the nature of Fishes who*
> *are cold and moyst by reason of*
> *their Element the water, yet they*
> *retain some little natural heat;*
> *so the ayr is then somewhat*
> *participating of some small*
> *quantity of heat, by reason of the*
> *Suns approach to the equinoctial*
> *point.*

Any concept of the more ancient legends
about Pisces clearly had vanished.

What we know about the constellation of Pisces today.

The constellation of Pisces is the 14th largest constellation in the sky, but the stars in Pisces are relatively faint.
Named for the Latin plural of the word for fish, Pisces occupies 889 square degrees of the sky. But even though it is a large constellation, the stars in it are so faint that it is challenging to see in the sky with the naked eye.

None of the stars in Pisces is brighter than 4th magnitude.

Although it has not been true throughout all of recorded history, at this point in time the Vernal Equinox, or the date when the Sun crosses the celestial equator into the Northern Hemisphere, is located in Pisces.

We know in the time of the ancients, the Vernal Equinox was in Aries.

Pisces can be found in the first quadrant of the Northern Hemisphere and covers a large V-shaped region. Its stars are so dim that despite the large area it covers, Pisces is difficult to pick out in the night sky.

Northern Hemisphere observers are able to see Pisces most clearly in early autumn. It is visible between latitudes 90 degrees and - 65 degrees and is best viewed between November 6 and November 9 around 9 PM. It is located northeast of Aquarius and Northwest of the constellation Cetus the Sea Monster.

Other constellations bordering Pisces are Triangulum, Andromeda, Pegasus, and Aries.

One of the key ways to identify Pisces is to find the **Circlet of Pisces**, also known as the "Head of the Western Fish," to the south of the **Great Square of Pegasus**. The eastern fish can be seen leaping upward to the east of the Square of Pegasus.

The main stars found in Pisces.

Alpherg also referred to as *Kullat Nunu* (or Eta Piscium in magnitude quantification) is the brightest star in Pisces.

Alpherg is a bright giant (G class) that is 294 light-years from Earth. It has a luminosity 316 times greater than that of our Sun.

The second brightest star in Pisces is a yellow giant about 130 light-years from Earth named **Gamma Piscium**. Devoid of a proper name, one of the unusual characteristics of Gamma Piscium is that it appears to be devoid of metal content or at least significantly metal-poor.

The third brightest star is actually a pair of white stars in close proximity known collectively as *Alrescha*, or "the cord" in Arabic. *Alrescha* (also referred to as Alpha Piscium as the magnitude indicator) illuminates the spot where the tails of the two fish are tied together.

A fourth star named *Fum al Samakah* (or Beta Piscium) comes from an Arabic phrase that means "Mouth of the Fish." *Fum al Samakah* has a magnitude of 4.53 and is about 492 light years from Earth.

Pisces' exoplanets.

Several exoplanets have been found in Pisces.

In 2014, astronomers found an exoplanet called GU Pisces b that orbits its star at an unbelievable two thousand times the distance between the Earth and our Sun. Given that distance, it takes this planet approximately 80,000 Earth years to go around its star one time.

GU Pisces b is indeed an exoplanet. But it is unlike any exoplanet previously known to us.

Also in 2014, when the Kepler telescope began its new mission, it discovered a super-earth called HIP 116454b in the constellation of Pisces that appears to be about 180 light-years from Earth.

In 2015, we launched a probe to HIP 116454b searching for extraterrestrial intelligence. To date, that search as turned up empty.

Deep sky objects of interest in the constellation of Pisces.

One Messier object, identified as Messier 74, is found in the Pisces constellation as well.

Messier 74 is a spiral galaxy located **between** the stars **Alpherg**, the brightest star in the constellation of Pisces, and **Hamal**, the brightest star in the neighboring constellation of Aries and also one of the brightest stars in the sky.

Little more than its existence and apparent location are known about Messier 74 to date.

When it comes to deep sky, Pisces remains mysterious.

Other particularly curious findings about Pisces.

An interesting note about the constellation of Pisces is that in 2014, the Hubble space telescope found a pair of bizarre galaxies they named Pisces A and Pisces B.

In 2016, astronomers found that data from the initial finding indicate these two dwarf galaxies used to exist by themselves, but over time they moved to a nearby group of galaxies—a process that accelerated star formation.

Researchers hope continued information about Pisces A and Pisces B from Hubble can enlighten scientists on what dwarf galaxies today may have looked like in the ancient past.

But possibly an even more fascinating note is that in 2013, researchers found this area of the galaxy (called NGC 660) experienced a **huge explosion**. It appeared this mega-explosion was caused by some type of energy streaming out of a black hole.

The first hypothesis was that a supernova, the explosion of a single star, had caused the massive explosion. But astronomers observed five separate locations with bright radio emissions near the galaxy's core, so a supernova was ruled out.

As of the writing of this book, our scientists are uncertain what triggered this massive explosion or series of explosions in the Pisces constellation.

Scientific probes into the constellation of Pisces during the last several decades of the 21st Century have found an exceptional number of anomalies. These findings have spurred a profusion of continued scientific investigation in this sector of space.

But so far, space exploration in Pisces has raised more questions than it has answered.

New insights into the meaning of Pisces?

In many ways, the ancient concept of Pisces is more similar to the modern one than it is for almost any other constellation.

The ancient themes of **Beauty** and **Sensuality** and **Sexual Love** tie in closely with our modern concept of Pisces, even though for most astrologers they are peripheral rather than the preeminent themes we think of.

The modern **fear of getting lost** *in* another person seems to oddly mirror the ancient fear of getting lost *from* the other. Though perhaps the differences are more indicative of modern man seeking a partner and yet fearing the bond, while the ancient concept assumed and embraced the bond of two.

The symbolism of **diving deep to the bottom** of the pond to **hide**. Those are very much Pisces in modern eyes.

But it seems clear there was either more to the myths or simply more myths about Pisces in antiquity than we have access to today.

It is, however, the science that may give the most kick in new understanding.

Not too surprisingly, it seems the more we study the constellation of Pisces, the more questions it raises. Instead of getting clarity, the harder we look, the murkier the view. That seems to be in direct alignment with the modern view of Piscean energy.

But what is unexpected in our scientific research from an astrologer's viewpoint is the finding there has been a recent massive explosion in Pisces. And this mega-explosion was caused by some type of energy streaming out of a black hole.

This information should be digested fully and totally by students of astrology because energy coming *in* from a black hole rather than energy being sucked *out* of a black hole is bound to have a three-dimensional effect some where.

Extremely powerful energy pouring *in* through our collective Pisces sub-conscious and into the dream states of many individual humans. It may seem invisible to us right now, we may be unaware or only remotely unaware of this activated dream-state, but Pisces energy always manifests in a concrete way eventually. It simply is never in a way or at a time we can schedule or direct.

So how does this "change" our modern concept of the Zodiac—or should it?

L ike most of the people who will take the time to read this book, I am a serious student of astrology. A large portion of the past six decades of my life have been spent reading every serious astrology book I could devour, studying with the best astrologers I could find, observing how charts and people "intersect" in life, and deeply contemplating the beautiful balance of the Twelve Signs of our Zodiac.

I suspect the same may be true for you.

I can only speak for myself here. Not for you—because your study and understanding may be very different.

But until very recently I had never heard of Ophiuchus. And although I had read about Antinous and Asclepius, it was only peripherally as curiosities from the distant past, unrelated to astrology. I was not aware how many other planets we now know exist or how many of them could potentially support life as we conceive it. I knew there was a Centaur connected to a sign of our zodiac in antiquity, but I did not know there were five zodiac signs connected with Centaurs in the ancient world. I didn't know Mercury is shrinking or that the constellation of Gemini is filled with doubles, Scorpio with multiples, and Pisces with anomalies. I did not realize how much of the ancient symbolism has been "lost" over time or how much is confirmed by our newest science. I did not know the oldest known star actually may pre-date the universe itself or that our most ancient star falls in the sign of Libra. I never considered how much, or possibly how many times, constellations and zodiac signs have changed over the eons.

And I certainly did not realize that there are thirteen constellations our Sun passes through on its annual journey. Now. Today.

Overlain on a well-structured and long-gathered
understanding is now this big pile of new facts.

And in the middle of digestion, a memory
arises about the "Dual Rulers" of Astrology.

In the Classical Western tradition,
Astrology is part Saturn and part Uranus. A
conundrum, or riddle, of sorts. But within all
riddles, there often lies a key.

On one hand, astrology is a creature of
SATURN. It is a Science rooted in tradition,
filled with highly structured and fixed rules
that is passed from one generation to the
next, century by century. The PAST is
preserved in a tightly guarded capsule of
sagacity distilled through ages of the old and,
at least hopefully, the wise. Like Saturn,
astrology defines the edges of the universe of
human experience and sets into human life
the motion of the ticking hands on the clock
of a limited mortal life.

And the on the other hand, astrology is a
creature of URANUS. It is an Art of sudden
insight and breathtaking breakthrough to the
FUTURE. At the speed of a flash of light, it
defies and explodes any containment and
catapults us through time and space to that
which is brand new and previously totally
unknown and even unknowable. With its
totally unpredictable and ever-changing

274

nature, it steps us up to the very edge of limitless immortality. Like Uranus, astrology takes us to unexpected places we never before have been.

And yet, the mystery of Astrology is the beautiful combination and balancing of these two energies.

Does the Zodiac change over time?

History shows us it does.

Should the Zodiac change over time? Or, maybe more to the point, will it change?

None of us mortals knows for sure. But I suspect the answer is yes to both.

In fact, it appears to be changing at this very moment.

Whether Ophiuchus shows up in our carefully calculated charts or not, at some point this very day Ophiuchus with rise and set on the Earth's horizon.

Someday we likely will see it more clearly. Clearly enough to both embrace it and chart a new course through an ever-changing and ever-contracting and ever-expanding universe.

Just like our most ancient ancestors did.

Parting thoughts from

the author.

This book is not written to advocate the position that the ancient past is superior to the present. It's not. And certainly even if it were in some ways, it is not in all ways.

Nor is this book written to advocate the position that science can tell us more than our mythology. I personally am unconvinced it can. Science simply tells us different kinds of things than mythology.

But we live today at a TRULY unique moment and vantage point.

We have access to information we never have had before—both from the distant past and from the cutting-edge "future" of scientific discoveries that are being made at such a dizzying pace even the smartest and most well-read of us have a difficult time keeping up.

There is no sign this rapid growth of information will halt any time soon.

Some of the information contained in this book, from one direction or the other, may give you an ah-ha moment or a flash of insight. It may explain something you have been wondering about. It may remind you of something you had forgotten. It may give you information you never have read about or considered possible. It may challenge what you previously have read or learned or believed.

And that is good. Any of it. Or all of it.

Only by looking back to our collective wisdom and embracing new facts can we grow.

And grow we indeed need to do.

In the end, whether Earth is taking a path of Devolution or Evolution is up to mankind. Collectively, and individually.
One by one of us. Day by day and hour by hour.

Moment by moment.

At the very least, let us remember the legends of the Moirai.

The Goddess of Fate may have spun the fabric of our lives before each of us were born—but the Great God of Ultimate Creation gives us latitude of **choice** and of **action** in every single moment of our mortal lives.

Let us live as though the planet depends on us. Because it does.

To the Highest and Best of us All,

Sonrisa East
14 April 2019

Author's Request.

If you found anything thought-provoking about this book, please take the time to leave a review on Amazon.

It may seem like a minor thing, but it is huge for a modern author. And it takes less than a minute-and-a-half.

Simply sign into your Amazon account and click on the title WHERE ALPHA MEETS OMEGA and then click the button that says "Leave a Review." As long as you have made one purchase on Amazon at some time in the past, your review will help make this book more easily seen in searches by other people.

And if you want to read about other astrological topics or if you would like to keep up with future releases, please join my V.I.P. readers' group at www.sonrisaeast.com.

Made in the USA
Middletown, DE
01 November 2023

41795332R00168